I'M A LEBOWSKI, YOU'RE A LEBOWSKI

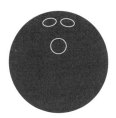

I'M A LEBOWSKI, YOU'RE A LEBOWSKI

20th Anniversary

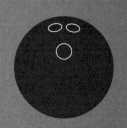

FOREWORD BY JEFF BRIDGES
AFTERWORD BY DAPHNE MERKIN

BLOOMSBURY
NEW YORK · LONDON · OXFORD · NEW DELHI · SYDNEY

Bloomsbury USA
An imprint of Bloomsbury Publishing Plc

1385 Broadway
New York
NY 10018
USA

50 Bedford Square
London
WC1B 3DP
UK

www.bloomsbury.com

First published 2007
This edition published 2018

ISBN: PB: 978-1-63557-125-7
ePub: 978-1-63557-126-4

LIBRARY OF CONGRESS CATALOGING-IN-PUBLICATION DATA

I'm a Lebowski, you're a Lebowski : life, The big Lebowski, and what have you /
Bill Green . . . {et al.}.—1st U.S. ed p. cm
ISBN: 978-1-63557-125-7
1. Big Lebowski (Motion Picture) I. Green, Bill– II. Title: I am a Lebowski, you are a Lebowski.
PN1997.B444I4 2007
791.43'72—dc22
2006103251

2 4 6 8 10 9 7 5 3 1

Design by Elizabeth Van Itallie
Printed and bound by LSC Communications, Crawfordsville, Indiana

To find out more about our authors and books visit www.bloomsbury.com. Here you will find extracts, author interviews, details of
forthcoming events, and the option to sign up for our newsletters.

Bloomsbury books may be purchased for business or promotional use. For information on bulk purchases please contact Macmillan
Corporate and Premium Sales Department at specialmarkets@macmillan.com.

They have neither our blessing nor our curse.

—The Coen brothers, in reference to the writing of this book

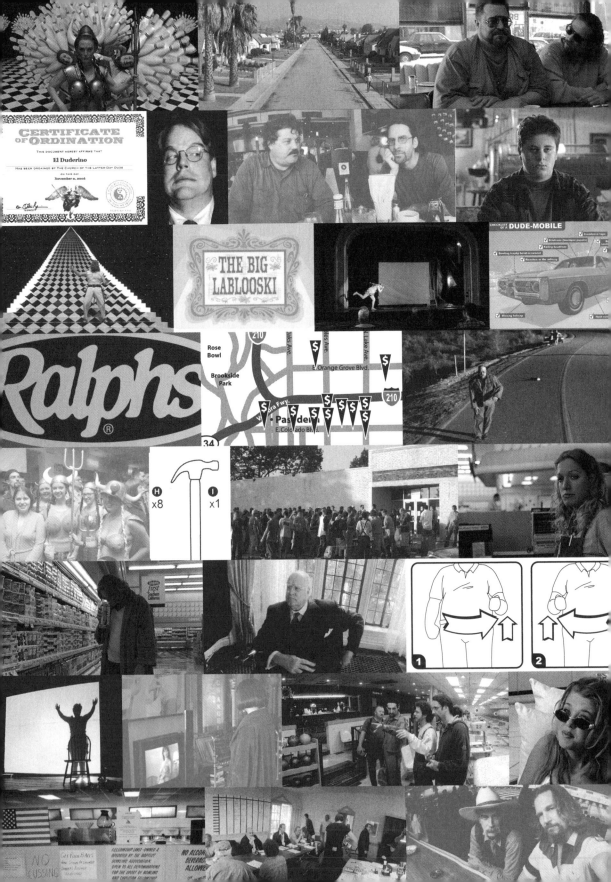

CONTENTS

INSTRUCTIONS FOR ENJOYING THIS BOOK

• •

Please take a minute to read through these seven simple steps to ensure that you get the most out of this book.

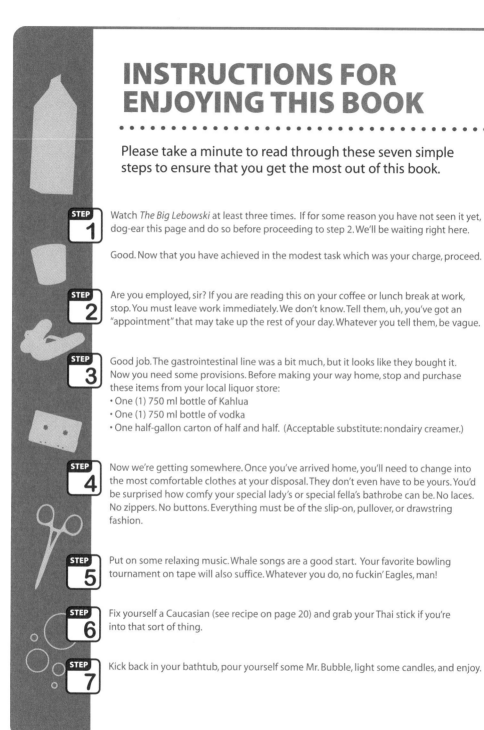

STEP 1 Watch *The Big Lebowski* at least three times. If for some reason you have not seen it yet, dog-ear this page and do so before proceeding to step 2. We'll be waiting right here.

Good. Now that you have achieved in the modest task which was your charge, proceed.

STEP 2 Are you employed, sir? If you are reading this on your coffee or lunch break at work, stop. You must leave work immediately. We don't know. Tell them, uh, you've got an "appointment" that may take up the rest of your day. Whatever you tell them, be vague.

STEP 3 Good job. The gastrointestinal line was a bit much, but it looks like they bought it. Now you need some provisions. Before making your way home, stop and purchase these items from your local liquor store:
• One (1) 750 ml bottle of Kahlua
• One (1) 750 ml bottle of vodka
• One half-gallon carton of half and half. (Acceptable substitute: nondairy creamer.)

STEP 4 Now we're getting somewhere. Once you've arrived home, you'll need to change into the most comfortable clothes at your disposal. They don't even have to be yours. You'd be surprised how comfy your special lady's or special fella's bathrobe can be. No laces. No zippers. No buttons. Everything must be of the slip-on, pullover, or drawstring fashion.

STEP 5 Put on some relaxing music. Whale songs are a good start. Your favorite bowling tournament on tape will also suffice. Whatever you do, no fuckin' Eagles, man!

STEP 6 Fix yourself a Caucasian (see recipe on page 20) and grab your Thai stick if you're into that sort of thing.

STEP 7 Kick back in your bathtub, pour yourself some Mr. Bubble, light some candles, and enjoy.

SAYING WHAT CAN'T BE SAID

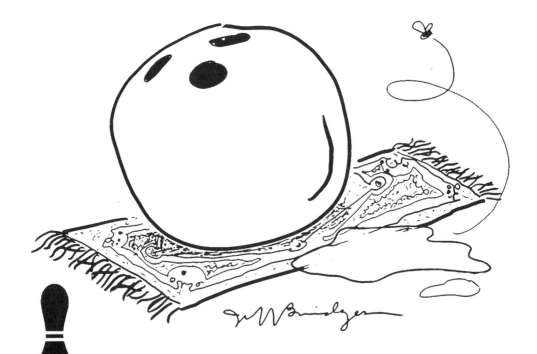

People often ask me if I'm surprised at the amount of attention *The Big Lebowski* has received over the past few years. They usually seem to expect me to say "yes," but my answer is always "no." What *surprises* me is that it didn't do as well as I thought it would when it first came out. It was so damn funny, and the Coen brothers had just won the Academy Award for *Fargo*—I thought people would flock to this thing. To tell you the truth, I was sort of disappointed. But now . . . well . . . I'm glad people are digging it . . . that it found its audience.

Diehard fans will sometimes ask me, "What is it about this movie? I can't figure it out—how come people like it so much?" Well, that one's a little tougher to answer. I usually point them toward the script, to what the Stranger says at the end of the movie. I think the Stranger's enjoyment of the story sums up what most people like about it:

THE STRANGER

. . . I don't know about you, but I take comfort in that. It's good knowin' he's out there, the Dude, takin' her easy for all us sinners. Shoosh. I sure hope he makes the Finals. Welp, that about does her, wraps her all up. Things seem to've worked out pretty good for the Dude'n Walter, and it was a purty good story, dontcha think? Made me laugh to beat the band. Parts, anyway. Course—I didn't like seein' Donny go. But then, I happen to know that there's a little Lebowski on the way. I guess that's the way the whole durned human comedy keeps perpetuatin' itself, down through the generations, westward the wagons, across the sands a time until—aw, look at me, I'm ramblin' again. Wal, uh hope you folks enjoyed yourselves.

What's great about that is how it says it all without really saying anything. Maybe that's one reason people dig the movie and are able to watch it over and over again. It's like picking up a kaleidoscope. You see something new each time.

Then there's *this* perspective. A few years ago I met a guy named Bernie Glassman. Bernie started an organization called the Zen Peacemakers and has founded a number of Zen centers in the United States. He calls his brand of Zen Farkatke Zen. He's a Jewish fella . . . a wonderful cat.

Anyway, we got to talking, and he said, "You know, a lot of folks consider the Dude a Zen Master." I said, "What are you talking about . . . Zen?" He said quite a few people had approached him wanting to chat about the Dude's Zen wisdom. I'd never heard of that.

I never thought of the Coen Brothers as Zen guys. They never talked about it. I don't think the word *Zen* was ever mentioned . . . or *Buddhism* . . . or *Judaism*, for that matter. I don't think of the Dude as a fancy spiritualist or anything like that. But I can see what these folks are talking about. There's enough room in the movie that a lot can be read into it.

I often take these little walks in the evening at sunset and listen to different things. Recently I played some Alan Watts, and it reminded me of my conversation with Bernie and how Zen relates to *Lebowski*. Watts says, "The whole art of poetry is to say what can't be said." I suppose that's true for any art, including filmmaking. He goes on to say that "Every poet, every artist feels when he gets to the end of his work, that there is something

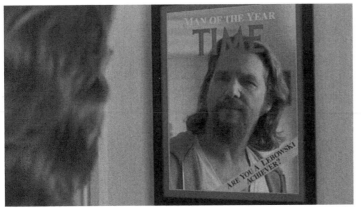

absolutely essential that was left out, so Zen has always described itself as a finger pointing at the moon." *The Big Lebowski* is a bit like that.

The guys who wrote this book say the Coens have kept clear of them entirely, and that tickles me. Like all of you reading this, I'd be interested to know what the Coen brothers think, but it's kind of beautiful that they don't want to say anything definitive. Let 'em be the *pointing fingers.*

For me, the Dude has a certain type of wisdom. I like to call it the "Wisdom of Fingernails": the wisdom that gives you the ability to make your hair and fingernails grow, your heart beat, your bowels move. These are things that we know how to do, but we don't necessarily know *how* we know how to do them, yet still we do them very well. And that to me is very Dude. It's not like he's a know-it-all, the Dude. He's not a guy who has figured out the way to be or anything like that, but he is comfortable with what he's got, and, as the Stranger says, things turn out pretty well for him. I guess we can all take comfort in that because . . . who knows? . . . things may turn out pretty well for us, too.

Recently someone asked me, "How would you feel at the end of your career if the role you were most famous for was the Dude?" "I'd be fucking delighted," I told him.

Abidingly,
Jeff Bridges

LOTTA INS, LOTTA OUTS, LOTTA WHAT HAVE YOUS

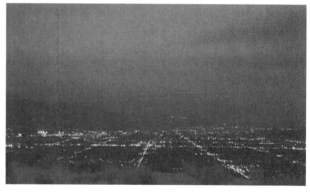

On a random weekend in June a few years back, we'd rented a booth to sell T-shirts at a tattoo convention. The convention was the worst kind: slow, but not slow enough to justify packing up and going home. It was held in a Holiday Inn conference room, and the entertainment consisted of two naked people hanging, suspended by their ass piercings*, from a contraption on the makeshift stage. Our booth happened to be the closest one to the stage. We were out of our element.

To pass the time, we engaged in our usual method of entertainment, quoting lines from *The Big Lebowski*. We'd had lots of practice. Whether breaking down gear after a show by our now-defunct band** or killing time vending at music festivals, we would

---

* To save you the trouble, a search for "ass piercing" on Google image search does no justice to what we endured.

** The Blue Goat War, our science fiction nerd-rock concept band. We occasionally wowed crowds of up to four or five people in coffeehouses and church basements.

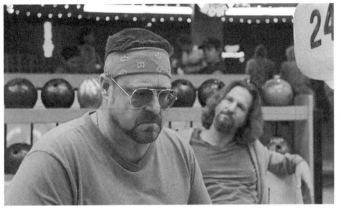

always find ways to work in a line. One person would yell, "You want a toe?" and someone would automatically respond with, "I can get you a toe! There are ways, Dude. You don't wanna know." Sometimes we even had enough restraint to leave the follow-up line up for grabs so that the lucky recipient would get to finish it off with, "Hell, I can get you a toe by three o'clock—with nail polish!" The more we watched the movie, the more we found ourselves quoting it. We found it to be a natural, zesty enterprise.

That day at the tattoo convention, we'd been trading lines for a while when, it being Saturday, one of us said, "Shabbos, Donny, is the Jewish day of rest."

And then a voice came out of nowhere: "That means I don't work, I don't drive a car, I don't fucking ride in a car, I don't handle money, I don't turn on the oven, and I sure as shit *don't fucking roll!*" We were befuddled. Had someone called Sobchak Security to take care

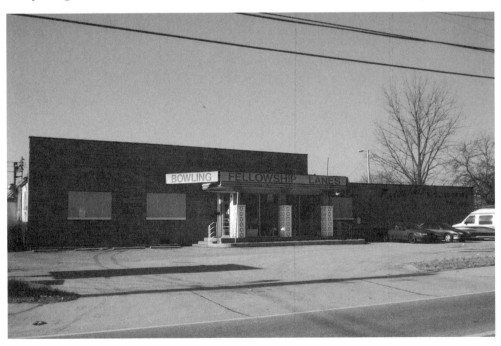

of the ass-people?* But it turned out the voice belonged to a guy in the booth next to us.

We turned to look at him and one of us chimed in with the obvious: *"Shomer Shabbos!"*

He raised a fist, Black Panther–style, and nodded. "Shomer fucking Shabbos."

As if we'd just completed a previously unknown ritual of initiation, we felt an instant bond. We began sharing quotes and trivia related to the movie. Eventually a few people walking by joined us. Soon we had a small group gathered around our booths, everyone trading lines and laughing. It was our first experience of spontaneous Lebowski, our first glimpse that there were others out there like us.

On Sunday afternoon we paused from packing up our booth to watch as they unhooked the ass-people for the final time. Confronted with that sight, a thought occurred to us: If these guys can have a tattoo convention, there's no reason—there's no fucking reason—why we can't have a *Big Lebowski* convention. We rode that wave of inspiration for about ten more seconds. By the time we stopped to take a breath, we'd managed to piece together what would become the basic formula for Lebowski Fest.

The idea was simple: Get fans of *The Big Lebowski* together in a bowling alley, and then turn them loose to bowl, drink White Russians, dress in costume, watch the movie together, and celebrate all things Lebowski.

If You Will It, Dude, It Is No Dream

Having the idea was one thing. Backing it up with time and energy was another. Who knew if anyone would actually come? So, being good Americans, we took a poll. When our friends said, "Mark it!" we scoured Louisville for the cheapest bowling alley we could find and hit secondhand shops in search of old bowling trophies to use as prizes.

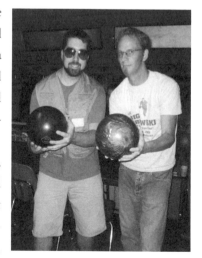

A beacon of virtue surrounded by a sea of strip clubs, liquor stores, and trailer parks, the Baptist-owned and -operated Fellowship Lanes opened its doors to the First Annual Big Lebowski What-Have-You Fest** on October 12, 2002. Giant signs at the entrance proclaimed,

---

* No.

** Yes, we know it's wrong to say "First Annual." Inaugural, please.

3

NO CUSSING and NO ALCOHOLIC BEVERAGES ALLOWED, and below these signs was a sign that stated, READ THE SIGNS!

Considering that the word *fuck* and its variations are spoken 281 times in the film and that "getting limber" is a central theme, it could not have been a stranger choice, but in true Dudelike fashion, the crowd largely ignored the rules and refused to let them spoil their fun. The dialogue quoting and bowling, and the trivia and costume contests gave the

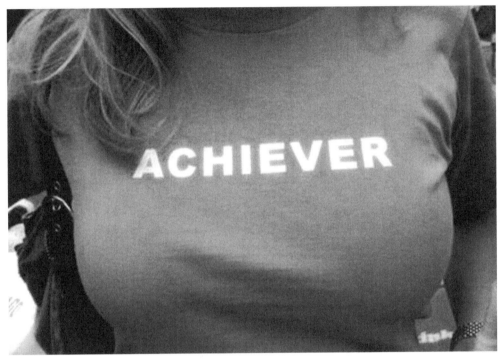

night the same sense of bonding we had felt at the tattoo convention. Although we'd expected a small crowd of about thirty friends, nearly 150 people showed up, including some who made the trek to Kentucky from as far away as Tucson and Buffalo.

Encouraged by that success, we opened the doors of LebowskiFest.com in December 2002. Word spread quickly as dedicated fans of *The Big Lebowski* began to realize they were not alone. These fans, who began to self-apply the name "Achievers," connected around the globe, trading lines of dialogue on the forum, spending hours in chat, and spreading the word through T-shirts and bumper stickers.

Lebowski Fest celebrated its five-year anniversary in the fall of 2006, and the phenomenon continues to grow. Lebowski Fest now has a world headquarters in Louisville, complete with five time-zone clocks and a rug that really ties the room together.

And Proud We Are of All of Them

Over the past few years we've been stupefied to discover just how much love there is for the Dude and his buddies, the movie that celebrates them, and the brilliant guys who dreamed it all up. Few experiences compare to an evening of throwing strikes and gutters among a group of like-minded Achievers. The common love of the film transcends age and race, religious and social boundaries.

The term *Achiever*, as it applies to fans of the movie, has a relatively short history. The term is taken, of course, from the Little Lebowski Urban Achievers (and proud we are of all of them). It started as an informal nickname on the LebowskiFest.com forum and has now become the preferred nomenclature for Lebowski fans everywhere. *Playboy* officially added it to the parlance of our times when they included it in the Tip Sheet of their November 2004 issue, alongside the equally noteworthy terms *Pole-*

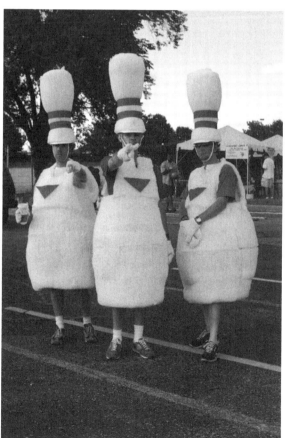

pox ("a rare but documented pole dancer's malady") and *Atkins Mouth* ("halitosis caused by low-carb diets").

Again being good Americans, we decided to make a T-shirt. We emblazoned the word *Achiever* in bold letters across the front and have shipped them to all parts of the world. People have sent us pictures of themselves in their Achiever shirts from places as far-flung as the Colosseum in Rome, an air base from our

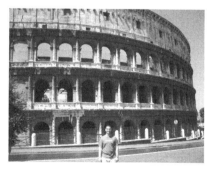

current situation in Iraq, a palace in India, and a suburb of Toledo. The entire collection of Achiever photos can be seen at LebowskiFest.com.

Ever Thus to Deadbeats

So why all the fuss? What is it about *The Big Lebowski* that has inspired so much interest and affection?

Well, Dude, we just don't know.

We interviewed the actors from the film, some of the real people who inspired the story, and fellow Achievers in search of the answer.

We hope you enjoy reading it as much as we enjoyed putting it together.

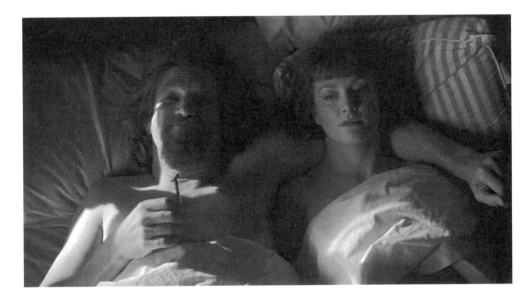

CHAPTER ONE

I WON'T SAY HERO, 'CAUSE WHAT'S A HERO?

A·bide *v*

1. to find somebody or something acceptable or bearable

2. to endure or withstand something (archaic)

3. to have the ability to say, "Fuck it. Let's go bowling"

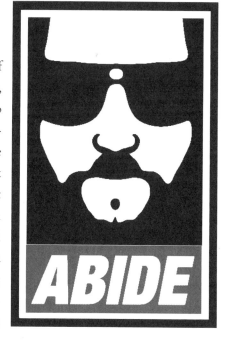

Way back in 1996, fresh off the set of the soon-to-be Oscar favorite *Fargo*, Joel and Ethan Coen were gearing up to shoot their next feature film. Written with a nod to classic noir crime films such as *The Big Sleep* and a wink to the Coens' growing, spoof-loving fan base, it was to be a film about a mistaken identity, a film about a kidnapping, a film about taking a stand against aggressors—but most of all, it was to be a film about, ahem, bowling? Throw in an aging hippie, a gun-toting Vietnam vet, a vain millionaire, and a few nihilists, and you've got what is now hailed as one of the most quotable cult films of the past two decades, *The Big Lebowski*.

You might have seen it in the theater, or maybe you caught part of it on cable a year or so later. If you're like most people, you had no idea what was going on. Even if you caught it from the beginning, you may still have felt like you had just tuned in to an episode of *Seinfeld* five minutes late, and every line seemed like an inside joke. It wasn't until the second or fifth time that you might have begun to see the layers of genius woven into *The Big Lebowski*.

And at the center of it all is the Dude, played by the man born for the role, Jeff Bridges.

It's not often that our culture presents us with a heroic icon who is also one of the laziest men of his time and place. Superman wears a cape, not a bathrobe. Neo has no trouble dodging a swarm of bullets, much less a coffee mug to the forehead. Batman never wrecked the Batmobile while looking for the joint he dropped. Nor does he care whether his cocktail is shaken or stirred. That's 007's thing, man. Even Homer Simpson has a job.

No, the Dude doesn't need all the fancy clothes, cars, or names. Just "the Dude." That's

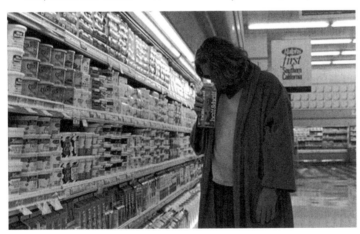

what people call him. And maybe this is wishful thinking, but it seems we all have a little bit of the Dude in us. Sitting right there next to that little bit of Elvis. If you enjoy bowling, the only "sport" that provides cup holders; if you've

ever looked the Man in the face and just said, "Fuck it"; if you've ever postdated a check for change—that's the Dude coming out of you. Feels good, doesn't it?

Quiz: How Dude Are You?

So just how Dude are you, anyway? Get out your number-two pencils and answer the following questions to discover how in touch you are with your inner Dude. Report back as soon as it's done.

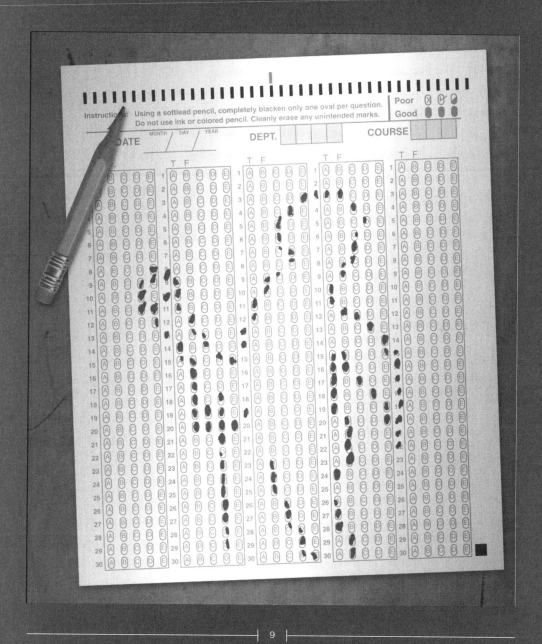

1. Are you employed, sir?

A) Yes

B) No

C) What day is this?

2. Do you have any Kahlua?

A) No, but I do have some watermelon schnapps

B) No, I'm fresh out

C) Does the pope shit in the woods?

3. What's your favorite Eagles album?

A) *Desperado*

B) *Ride the Lightning*

C) I hate the fucking Eagles

4. What do you do in your free time?

A) Balance my checkbook

B) Occupy various administration buildings

C) Bowl, drive around, the occasional acid flashback

5. What is the smallest check you've ever written?

A) $100 and up

B) $0.70 to $99.99

C) $0.69 and under

6. Identify this small woodland mammal ————————

A) Beaver

B) Ferret

C) Marmot

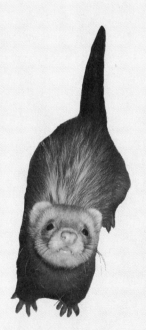

7. What cassette is in your Walkman right now?

A) I have an iPod

B) Creedence

C) *Venice Beach League Playoffs 1987/Bob*

8. What is your primary form of ID?

A) Driver's license

B) Expired student ID

C) Ralphs Card

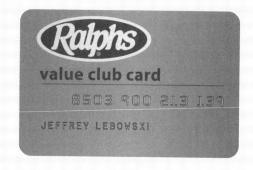

9. What color is your vehicle?

A) My Hummer is yellow

B) Blue

C) Green with rust coloration

10. When do you pay your rent?

A) When you own, it's called a *mortgage*

B) The tenth

C) Far out, man

Tally up your score:

For each A) answer, you get 0 points

For each B) answer, give yourself 21 points

For each C) answer, give yourself 42 points

How Dude are you:

0–105 = You're being very un-Dude

106–210 = You are the walrus

211–419 = I dig your style, man

420 = You abide

So how'd you do? Now that you have a feel for your level of Dudeness, here are some tips for Dude-ifying your everyday life.

How to Dude-ify Your Office Space

Beyond the obvious (and job-threatening) stunts such as putting White Russians in the water cooler and magic brownies in the break room, there are some more subtle ways to Dude-ify your work space.

- Every so often when your boss comes by with a new assignment, look at him blankly and say, "I'm sorry, I wasn't listening." If that one gets you hassled, try "That's fucking interesting, man."
- They say "casual Friday," but do they really mean it? Wear your bathrobe and jellies to work.
- Before leaving for vacation, change your incoming voicemail message to say, "The Dude is not in. Leave a message after the beep . . . Takes a minute."
- Download a whale screen saver. For connoisseurs, we recommend the ones with the relaxing sounds of the humpback whale song over lapping water.

Whale Sounds

In the late sixties, around the time Jeff Dowd and the Students for a Democratic Society were occupying various administration buildings, a group of whale biologists dropped a microphone into the ocean. Led by Roger Payne, the researchers captured a dazzling variety of moans and groans whose melodies were as haunting as they were surprising. Within a few years, Payne's recordings made their way to vinyl, and the album he produced, *Songs of the Humpback Whale,* became a bestseller at music stores across the United States and Europe. The humpbacks were the first cetaceans to go platinum.

Having studied the songs extensively since that time, scientists now know quite a lot about the "songster of the sea." According to the ocean rangers over at the TV show *Nature,* for example, both male and female humpbacks can produce sounds, but only the males produce long, organized songs with distinct themes and melodies. Songs typically last ten to fifteen minutes and a male might repeat the same song without pause for hours.

Humpback whale songs are some of the loudest sounds made by any animal. The lowest notes in their songs can cross dozens and possibly hundreds of miles of ocean water. As Roger Payne once put it, "When you are swimming and hear a humpback whale singing very close to you underwater, you sometimes feel you may not be able to stand the intensity of the sound. It is as though someone put their palms firmly against your chest and vibrated you until your whole skeleton was humming."

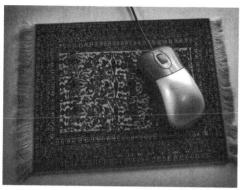

- If you don't have room for the real thing, a rug mouse pad can really tie a work space together.
- Lend the cleaning staff a hand—put some Mr. Bubble in the toilets.
- Save up to $0.69 by pinching some half and half (or nondairy creamer) from the break room for those postwork White Russians.
- Add a few bowling trophies to prove to the square community that you're not a bum after all.
- Two words: tiki bar!

If any of these suggestions lead to your termination, congratulations! On your way out be sure to notify your escort that the boss said you could take any computer in the house. Well, enjoy.

How to Dude-ify Your Car

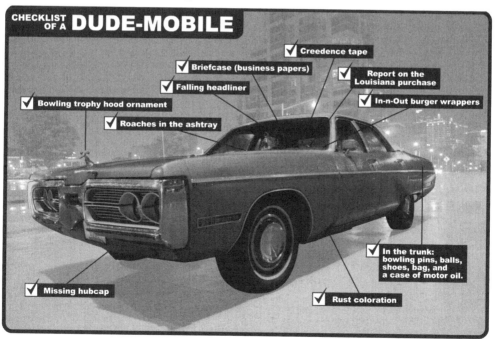

CHECKLIST OF A **DUDE-MOBILE**

- Creedence tape
- Briefcase (business papers)
- Report on the Louisiana purchase
- Falling headliner
- In-n-Out burger wrappers
- Bowling trophy hood ornament
- Roaches in the ashtray
- In the trunk: bowling pins, balls, shoes, bag, and a case of motor oil.
- Missing hubcap
- Rust coloration

How to Dude-ify Your Living Space

- Always refer to your apartment, house, or what have you as a bungalow.
- Married or not, leave the toilet seat up. You never know when you'll be forced to take another look.
- Your bungalow must be secure in order to keep nihilists and thugs from entering your home. Make sure to barricade your door by nailing a two-by-four to your hardwood floor. Post a sign that says, THIS IS A PRIVATE RESIDENCE, MAN.
- Don't forget a poster of Nixon bowling, aka the Big Milhouski. Crook or no crook, that creep can roll, man!

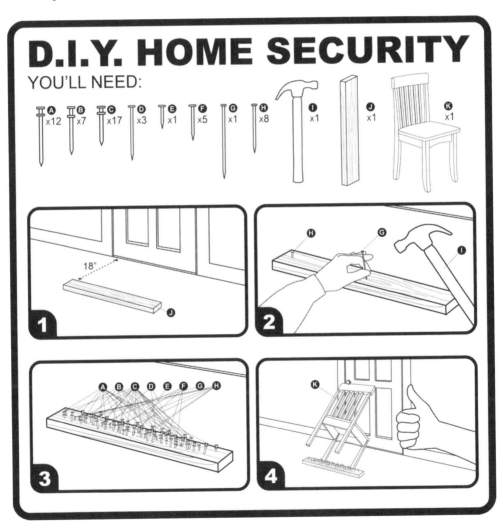

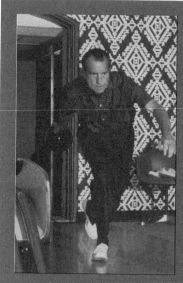

The Big Milhouski

This image is of President Nixon bowling at the White House basement lanes on September 27, 1971. The White House staff made efforts to publicize Nixon's "avid" bowling interest, staging photo ops that presented the president as a regular individual with a regular interest that other Americans shared. The lanes were a gift to President Truman in 1947 but were moved from the basement of the West Wing to the Executive Office Building in 1955; fourteen years later, Nixon had a one-lane alley built for himself, the First Lady, and his close friends.

- And then, of course, the rug—unless your household happens to include an unhousebroken cat, dog, or Asian American. Whenever you have visitors, remind them frequently that the rug really ties the room together.

- When lying in the tub, always keep within arm's reach a bottle of Mr. Bubble, candles, roach clip, a marmot trap, and both of your toilet brushes.

At Least It's an Ethos

The Big Lebowski contains references to such a multitude of ideologies and doctrines that you might think it was written by a philosophy major.* Judaism's three thousand years of beautiful tradition are poetically captured in Walter's rantings about Shomer Shabbos. The nihilists' firm belief in nothing shares a lane with Smokey's pacifism. The sheriff of Malibu is clearly a fucking fascist, and say what you will about the tenets of National Socialism—at least it's an ethos. A closer inspection of Bunny and her friend Sherry reveals their . . . where were we? Oh, yeah, their hedonism. Maude's feminism makes most men uncomfortable: *vagina*. To say that the Stranger's name is a nod to existentialism might seem like a bit of a stretch, but did you ever notice the copy of Sartre's *Being and Nothingness* on the Dude's bedside table? And Christianity? Jesus. You said it, man.

* You'd be right. Ethan Coen earned a degree in philosophy from Princeton.

But more than anything else, fans of the film have noticed a certain Zenlike, Buddhist quality to the Dude. Many times we've looked at the Dude and seen a slightly thinner, slightly hairier version of the Buddha. Or, as we like to call him, the Duddha. The Buddha teaches that life is suffering and that the only way to escape this suffering is to follow the eightfold path. This is the Duddha's (or El Duddharino's) way.

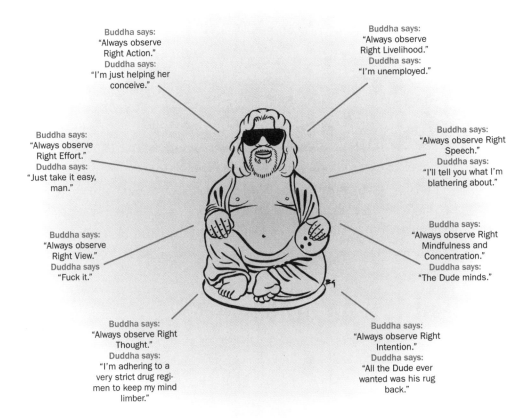

Buddha says:
"Always observe
Right Action."
Duddha says:
"I'm just helping her
conceive."

Buddha says:
"Always observe
Right Livelihood."
Duddha says:
"I'm unemployed."

Buddha says:
"Always observe
Right Effort."
Duddha says:
"Just take it easy,
man."

Buddha says:
"Always observe Right
Speech."
Duddha says:
"I'll tell you what I'm
blathering about."

Buddha says:
"Always observe
Right View."
Duddha says
"Fuck it."

Buddha says:
"Always observe Right
Mindfulness and
Concentration."
Duddha says:
"The Dude minds."

Buddha says:
"Always observe Right
Thought."
Duddha says:
"I'm adhering to a
very strict drug regi-
men to keep my mind
limber."

Buddha says:
"Always observe Right
Intention."
Duddha says:
"All the Dude ever
wanted was his rug
back."

Duderonomy: Rules to Live by, and Sometimes Break

Just as we were attempting to wrap our heads around this whole Eastern Duddha thing, we were contacted by a fellow Achiever named Oliver Benjamin. Oliver, who sometimes self-applies the name "Olly Lama," is the founder of the Church of the Latter-Day Dude, also known as Dudeism. At his official website, dudeism.com, you can connect with other Dudeists, get Dudeist self-help, and even become an official Dudeist Priest! Following the "instant online ordination," anyone can legally perform all varieties of religious ceremonies in most U.S. states (check with your local county clerk, as laws vary).

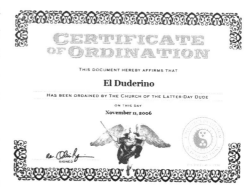

Born in Los Angeles and currently residing in Thailand, Oliver is in a special position to dig the Eastern-meets-Western aspects of *The Big Lebowski*. Dudeism draws its inspirations from the hodgepodge of world philosophies peppered throughout the film. The rules below, for instance, are based on the Judeo-Christian Bible's Deuteronomy, the section that deals with laws you need to follow to live life properly and that, as Oliver claims, "is hopelessly outdated. Here's the Dudeo-Coen version: *Duderonomy*."

BOOK 1

1. Thou shalt always use fresh creamer when preparing the sacrificial beverage. To ensure its freshness, it must be sniffed and even sampled before purchase. If it is unclean, put it back.

2. Ideally, half and half shall be used in preparing the sacrificial beverage. Failing this, milk, and, under the most dire of circumstances, nondairy creamer.

3. When confronted by vicious thugs demanding money, give it to them. If you don't have it, employ humor to lighten the situation. Do not under any circumstances try to fight back by hurling your bowling ball at them.

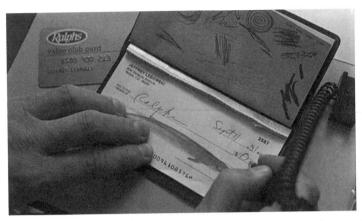

4. Always write checks whenever possible, as your cash is limited and you never know when you might have to pay off roving bands of heathen nihilists.

5. When discussing a matter of grave importance, or even of trifling idiocy, always make sure to employ expletives as much as possible to prove your heartfelt honesty and conviction. To ensure your Dudeness, all out-of-control, manic discussions should be followed with entreaties to "just take it easy, man."

6. If an adversary is clearly too uptight to see things from your perspective, don your sunglasses and intone, "Fuck it." Then take something of fair value from his house as you depart.

7. Employ comfortable furnishings in your home such as reclining chairs, scented candles, Persian rugs, and fanciful minibars with ironic posters of former adversaries. Your house is your temple, and your temple should be well tied together.

8. Always honor your landlord. Do your best to pay the rent on time. Failing that, indulge his artistic ambitions regardless of how utterly misguided they might be.

9. Never have an outward-opening door on your house.

10. When confronted by a large man with a gun who demands that you mark it zero, oblige him. Otherwise you risk entering a world of pain. Ideally he will get his comeuppance from the League for contravening a number of its bylaws.

BOOK 2

1. Never trust wealthy, successful people you hardly know who want to engage you in shady undertakings.

2. Money is the root of all evil. It's also the root of all good stories, so hooray for money.

3. A plan referred to as "foolproof" is often proved foolish.

4. If you're a pederast, identify yourself with a major religion in order to throw people off the scent.

5. Respect everyone's point of view. It's just, like, their opinion, man.

6. Always remember interesting turns of phrase that you hear so that you can employ them

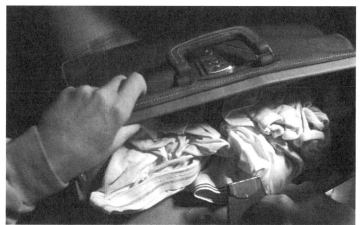

in completely unrelated situations later and convincingly sound as if you know what you're talking about.

7. The ringer cannot look empty.

8. Make sure to always use the proper pronoun. No one uses the editorial or royal "we" in everyday exchange unless they're trying to hide something.

9. Never park in a handicapped space if you've got a million dollars in the trunk of your car. In fact, never leave a million dollars in the trunk of your car, especially if your car is in lousy condition.

10. If a doctor is referred to as "thorough," harbor some reservations about visiting him. Unless, of course, you enjoy that sort of thing.

11. When confronted by unfortunate circumstances, forget about it. You can't be worrying about that shit. Life goes on.

12. Always protect your sacrificial beverage, even in times of severe duress.

13. Whenever possible, try to get paid in cash in order to avoid getting bumped up into a higher tax bracket.

CAREFUL, MAN, THERE'S A BEVERAGE HERE!

WHITE RUSSIAN
> 2 oz vodka
> 1 oz Kahlua
> half and half (suitable substitutes: milk or nondairy creamer)

Served over ice in a rocks glass.

BLACK RUSSIAN
> ¾ oz coffee liqueur
> 1½ oz vodka

Served over ice in a rocks glass.

RED RUSSIAN
> 1½ oz vodka
> ¾ oz Heering cherry liqueur

Stir over ice cubes in a mixing glass, strain into an aperitif glass, and serve.

WHITE TRASH RUSSIAN
> Vodka
> Yoo-Hoo

Drink half a bottle of Yoo-Hoo, refill with vodka, shake, and enjoy.

RUSSIAN
> Vodka (Jeff Bridges's preferred beverage)

Serve over ice in rocks glass, or just drink out of the bottle

BOOK 3

1. Freedom is great. Many young men have died facedown in the muck to protect our freedoms. Nevertheless, one should still be courteous and keep one's voice down in a family restaurant.

2. Unless you're a high-ranking member of society, don't expect too much from the police.

3. Sometimes not having an ethos is an ethos in itself. Usually it's a bad one, though.

4. Never go into a tournament with a negative attitude.

5. Try not to use so many cusswords. Unless they're near and dear to your heart, in which case, fuck it.

6. Make sure the window of your car is rolled down before ejecting a burning object. You probably shouldn't drink beer and drive, either, even though it might come in useful to extinguish the burning object.

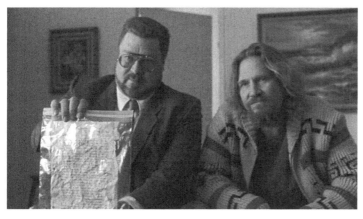

7. When strange men show up at your house accusing you of a crime and brandishing evidence, it is best that you feign mental illness and don't say a peep.

8. What happens when one fucks a stranger in the ass is not always what one might think will happen, nor what is necessarily fair or just to any of the concerned parties.

9. Never trust a known pornographer to whom any sizeable sum of money is owed.

10. Never trust a cab driver who enjoys listening to the Eagles.

BOOK 4

1. If you are a man of modest means and charisma and a rich, beautiful woman wants to have sex with you, don't question her motives until after the act is over.

2. Avoid living in the past, even if memories can be beautiful and remind you of a time you once enjoyed.

3. Though the man in the black pajamas might be a worthy adversary, you should avoid him whenever possible. Especially if he's so easily avoided. Choose instead to cling to the tree of life.

4. Just because you're bereaved doesn't make you a sap. Keep your wits about you, even when you're bummed out.

5. Take 'er easy for all the sinners of the world, Dude. Abide. And amen.

Duderonomy appears courtesy of Oliver Benjamin; www.dudeism.com.

Dude Libs

Lebowski Mad Libs, or what happens when you find a stranger in the Alps.
(You know, for kids!)

1. Noun _____

2. Adjective _____

3. Adjective _____

4. Adjective _____

5. Noun (plural)_____

6. Noun (plural) _____

7. Noun _____

8. Verb (present tense) _____

9. Adjective _____

10. Adjective _____

11. Adjective_____

12. Noun _____

13. Adjective _____

14. Noun _____

15. Adjective _____

16. Noun _____

Sheriff of Malibu County Scene

SHERIFF: Is this your only ID?

DUDE: I know my rights, man.

SHERIFF: You don't know **(1)**, Lebowski.

DUDE: I want a **(2)** lawyer, man. I want Bill Kunstler, man . . . or Ron Kuby.

SHERIFF: Mr. Treehorn tells us that he had to eject you from his garden party, that you were **(3)** and **(4)**.

DUDE: Jackie Treehorn treats **(5)** like **(6)**.

SHERIFF: Mr. Treehorn draws a lot of water in this town, Lebowski. You don't draw **(7)**, Lebowski. Now, we got a nice, quiet little beach community here, and I aim to keep it nice and quiet. So let me make something plain. I don't like you **(8)** around bothering our citizens, Lebowski. I don't like your **(9)** name, I don't like your **(10)** face, I don't like your **(11)** behavior, and I don't like you, **(12)**. Do I make myself clear?

DUDE: I'm sorry, I wasn't listening. [*Sheriff throws coffee cup, hits Dude in forehead.*] Ow! **(13)** fascist!

SHERIFF: Stay out of Malibu, Lebowski! Stay out of Malibu, **(14)**! Keep your ugly **(15)** goldbricking **(16)** out of my beach community!

CHAPTER TWO

PARTS, ANYWAY. THE ACTORS AND THEIR ROLES

It's amazing how far you can get by simply asking. At least that was the consensus around the Lebowski Fest World Headquarters during the writing of this book. One week we'd be thinking, "Wouldn't it be amazing to speak to John Turturro?" and the next thing we knew, the Jesus himself would be calling us at three p.m. We would find ourselves huddled around a really bad speakerphone chatting with people who, to us, are larger than life, swapping favorite lines and bouncing theories back and forth about why this movie has such a hold on so many people. One thing rang true in most of the interviews: we were not worthy. And most of the people on the receiving end of our uber-nerd-like questions knew this. But nonetheless they were all very kind and, instead of crushing us like grapes, gave us all the time and stories we could ask for.

We'd seen the "Special Features" sections on enough DVDs to expect all of the actors to have nice things to say about each other and working with the Coen brothers. But we were in no way prepared for the level of enthusiasm we encountered: *Gushing* might be a better word. The actors appreciated each other's brilliant performances, but more than anything else they appreciated the atmosphere the Coen brothers created on the set. As John Turturro put it, "The thing with the Coen brothers is that they're so disciplined that they allow you to be

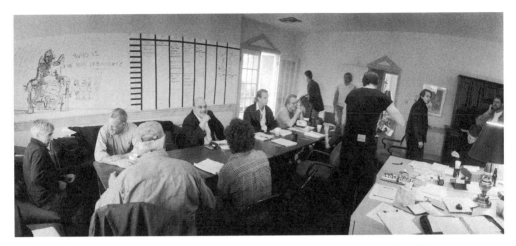

free, because they've done so much work." And that was a sentiment echoed by everyone we interviewed. The Coens are so prepared that the actors are free to do just that: act.

In fact, everyone we interviewed raved so much about working with the Coen brothers that it almost seemed suspicious. (Did the brothers have dirt on *everyone?*) That was until we were lucky enough to speak with a member of the crew, Sam Sarkar. Sam worked as a sound tech under the direction of the Coens' longtime sound director, Alan Byer. "The whole thing was like going to film school for three years," he says. "It was literally like watching amazing live theater every day." Although it's been almost ten years since the shoot, Sarkar has no trouble telling story after story of how fun it had been on the set— from the day they filmed Turturro's Jesus sequences and no one could keep a straight face ("Bridges and Goodman had to turn their backs to John during his close-ups so they wouldn't start laughing"), to the day they filmed Donny's ashes being blasted from an air cannon, to the day they filmed the final confrontation with the nihilists, when Walter's bowling ball went astray and ricocheted around the bowling alley parking lot.

"And actually that was the year that Joel and Ethan won the Oscar for *Fargo*," Sarkar says. "And this is the great thing about them, too: they were just so nonplussed about it, in a way, because they thought if anything the movie that probably would have been a contender was something like *Miller's Crossing* or *Barton Fink*. So they came in the next morning [after winning multiple Academy Awards] and they were in the breakfast line, and everybody was ecstatic, and they were just shrugging: 'Why *Fargo?*' They were happy about it, but they didn't quite get it. They were great. It was really amazing to watch."

JEFF BRIDGES

Name: Jeff Bridges

Character: The Dude

Born: Los Angeles, December 4, 1949

Select Filmography: *The Door in the Floor, Seabiscuit, The Contender, The Fisher King, The Fabulous Baker Boys, Starman, Tron, The Last Picture Show*

Trivia: In addition to acting, Jeff is also an accomplished photographer, musician, and artist.

Bums: First, can you tell us how you initially got involved with the movie?

Jeff Bridges: I had heard, or they told me, that they had written a script for me. And I was a big fan of theirs—I loved *Blood Simple*. And when they finally gave me the script, I was kind of surprised in a wonderful way. I loved the story and everything, but it was quite unlike anything I'd done before, and it seemed like they had spied on me at a couple of high school parties I was at. Like they were stalking me or something.

Bums: Did you do anything in particular to prepare for being the Dude?

JB: Just what I normally do in preparation for a movie. Often I go into my own closet and think about different clothes that I have that this guy could have, and I invite the

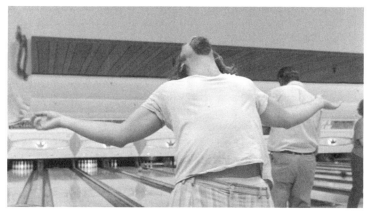

wardrobe person over. Found a lot of stuff in my closet that worked for the Dude. Found those jelly shoes, those were mine.

Bums: Were those stunt joints in the film?

JB: Those were stunt joints. I made that mistake earlier in my career where you're doing a drunk scene or a high scene and you decide to partake in something to give you the feeling. That's fine for the first couple of takes, but you've got

> **Those were stunt joints.**

to sustain that all day long, and there are other things besides just giving the impression that you're ripped. You know, the Coen brothers have a lot of witty lines, and you've really got to be on your game. And I decided to use what actors call "sense memory." I know what that feels like, so I just remembered.

Bums: What was it like filming a movie with the Coen brothers?

JB: Well, just the fact that you're working with two people directing you. They call them the Coen brothers. I was concerned about that, getting direction from two different sources, and what if they argued about it. I mean, I love my brother Beau, but imagining directing something together is . . . kind of a crazy thought. And these guys were so in tune with each other that at one point I asked them, "How do you guys do it?"

And they said they work it all out in the writing. By the time they get to shooting it, they are all in agreement about what it's supposed to be like. I think the only time that they disagreed on anything was in the scene in the Dude's dream, the scene where I'm going through the bowling pin chorines' legs, and I'm about to hit the bowling pins with my head. Just as we were about to shoot, Joel said, "So you're about to hit the pins and you squint your eyes, and you think it's going to be kind of a painful experience, and then you hit the pins."

And Ethan came up and said, "Oh, really? I thought he would be kind of happy when he hit the pins." And Joel said, "Really? I thought he would be grimacing." And Ethan said, "Really? I thought it would be more of a happy thing."

And they said, "Well, let's just do it both ways." And so that was the big argument.

Bums: What was it like when John Turturro showed up in the purple jumpsuit the day they filmed the Jesus stuff?

JB: He had worked with the Coen brothers before, and I had worked with him prior to that in *Fearless*—so it was kind of like showing up to a jam session or something. And he comes in and he looks so fuckin' great, and he was amazing in that part.

Often I'll be watching TV, and I'll be hitting the clicker, and if a movie of mine will come on, I'll rarely get hooked in cause I've seen the thing. But *The Big Lebowski*, when that gets on, I'll always say, "I'll just watch Turturro . . . I'll hang in till Turturro shows up." And then once he's there, I'll say, "I'll just watch until he gets to the part about sticking the gun up the ass."

Bums: Do you ever bowl?

JB: Probably the last time I bowled was in *The Big Lebowski*. Which is kind of ironic because you don't see me bowl in *The Big Lebowski*. But we trained extensively for the bowling scenes.

I remember a funny story of our bowling coach, Barry Asher—the last shot of the movie is him pitching a strike, isn't it? Barry was a champion bowler, and he had an assistant there with him, and they were both helping us—me, John, and Steve Buscemi—learn how to bowl.

And I was trying to figure out how the Dude's preparation would be before he threw the ball. I thought it would be an Art Carney type of thing. Remember how Art Carney, whatever he was gonna do, he'd take hours in preparation? And so I asked Barry, "Do you think the Dude would do something like that?"

And Barry's assistant laughed and looked up at Barry. And Barry proceeded to tell me that he would get up and his preparation would take minutes—ten minutes, sometimes, in the middle of a tournament.

Playing my tunes to a sea of Dudes. It was a very dreamlike, wonderful scene. It was great.

Because in bowling, as in many things in life, the pins are down even before you cock your hand back to pitch the ball. It's all mental attitude, kind of a Zen and the art of bowling thing.

And so he's waiting for his mind to get in the right place before he winds up, and sometimes his mind wouldn't be there, and so he kept waiting and doing different things, ticks and twitches, to get it there. And finally he had to actually go to a doctor and work on it.

And so I said, "Well, how do you throw it now?" And he said, "Now I just get up and throw the fucking ball."

Last time we talked, you guys asked me, "What parts of the Dude are Jeff Bridges?"

And my answer was that I kind of aspire to that wisdom that he has, tapping into the way it is and digging what's there. Just getting out of the way.

Bums: When you went to the Lebowski Fest in L.A., somebody asked you what you thought of it, and in a very Dude way you said, "It all seems like some kind of weird dream I'm having." That was one of the best things we'd heard in a long time.

JB: Well, I said that—to kind of contextualize it—one of my favorite songs is that little song, "Row, row, row your boat, gently down the stream/merrily, merrily, merrily, merrily, life is but a dream." That's probably a favorite of the Dude's, I would imagine. Looking at life as this dream that we're having. I'm just laughing at that thing you told me that I said. It certainly sounds like the things that I often say, especially in a situation where you get up onstage and I'm playing my tunes to a sea of Dudes. It was a very dreamlike, wonderful scene. It was great.

I just love it. I'm so grateful to you guys that you've kept this fire burning to see how much we can get out of this movie. And it's kind of like perpetual motion or something. You know, everybody kind of says, "Yeah! Yeah!" and you get swept up in this thing and you see more and more beauty in it.

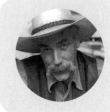

The Stranger Says . . .
"Mark it, Dude." The Dude is never actually seen bowling.

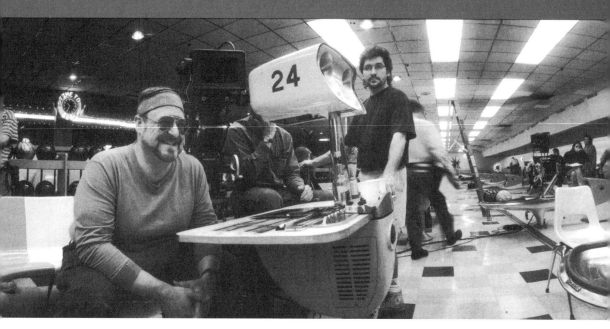

JOHN GOODMAN

Name: John Goodman

Character: Walter Sobchak

Born: St. Louis, June 20, 1952

Select Filmography: *Monsters, Inc.*; *O Brother, Where Art Thou?*; *Roseanne*; *The Hudsucker Proxy*; *Barton Fink*; *Raising Arizona*; *Revenge of the Nerds*

Trivia: John has hosted *Saturday Night Live* twelve times.

John Goodman: [*answering phone*] Lebowski Fest?

Bums: A good day to you, sir.

JG: Lebowski Fest. What do you bastards want?

Bums: We want the money.

JG: I'm out.

Bums: Thanks for taking the time to do this. We really appreciate it. To start, how did you meet the Coen brothers?

JG: I got a call to go in on a film called *Raising Arizona*—it was the funniest thing I'd ever read in my life. There was a very laid-back audition, and we seemed to hit it off—I could be fooling myself—but anyway I got the job, and I liked the way they worked.

Bums: Out of all your Coen brothers roles, do you have a favorite?

JG: Yeah, Walter. Actually I think that's my favorite thing I've ever done in my life.

Bums: Did you do any sort of preparation for the role of Walter?

JG: No, I just did what they pretty much told me to do. I wanted a different type of beard, but they insisted on the Gladiator—what they call the Chin Strap—and I thought that went well with the flattop.

Bums: Did you meet John Milius [one of the inspirations for Walter, see page 119]?

JG: No, man. He'd probably intimidate me—well, cocker spaniels intimidate me.

Bums: The relationship between the Dude and Walter is at the heart of the film. How would you describe their relationship?

> # Dipshit with a nine-toed woman. Where are you going to get another line like that, my friend?

JG: Weirder than duck lib.* They both share a love of bowling. Dude has a rather, let's say, Eastern approach to bowling. Walter is strictly Manifest Destiny. If that makes any sense. In nuevo Hebrew.

Bums: What was the toughest moment during the shooting of *The Big Lebowski*?

---

* We're not sure what duck lib is, and the Google doesn't know, either.

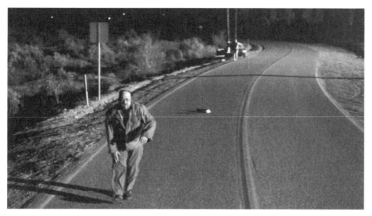

JG: I had to lie to the brothers one time. I rolled my motorcycle, and I told them I'd slipped in my swimming pool. They didn't need me that much that day anyway, and so they put me in a house and lined me up with Demerol. My ankle swelled up to the size of a balloon. Lying to the boys, I felt bad about that.

And man, that night when I had to wreck the 'vette. They didn't tell me that they bought the neighborhood out. We had to do the scene with Little Larry, and then I had to go out and wreck the car, and I thought that these people were going to be in their houses being rudely awakened by a movie crew with me screaming, "This is what happens when you fuck a stranger in the ass!" I was seriously worried about it. And Joel and Ethan never bothered to tell me that they bought the neighborhood out. I was scared to death to go out and start screaming obscenities in the middle of this middle-class neighborhood. And then I caught on because there were no blinking lights and no complaints or anything. But how much fun is it to wreck a 'vette like that [*laughing*]? I'm the luckiest boy in the world.

Bums: Do you have a favorite line from the movie or a favorite scene?

JG: "Nihilists. Say what you want about the tenets of National Socialism, at least it's an ethos." "We believe in nothing." And then the little machine voice in the background: "We understand that one of your colleagues, a Mr. Walter Sobchak . . ." What did I call him? A something with a nine-toed woman—

Bums: Dipshit.

JG: Dipshit with a nine-toed woman. Where are you going to get another line like that, my friend? Just give them the money, Walter.

Bums: We're not fucking around here, man.

JG: It's really cool now because, well, nobody sets out to make a cult movie, unless you're Roger Corman. But it's very rewarding now to have kids come up and quote stuff to me. It's very pleasing. Now, if it was *The Flintstones*, I would have put a nine-millimeter in my mouth a long time ago. But this one I don't seem to mind. It just touches me that people come up to me today, especially younger guys—rarely chicks—and tell me how much they dig it. Then they go into such arcana about it, you know they really listen.

Bums: What do you think it is about *The Big Lebowski* that resonates so strongly with people?

JG: It's just so well fucking written. It's the writing. The writing, the detail . . . I'm not going to start making up words here, but it's the noir quality of it . . . Oh, crap, it's just funny. It's smart and it's funny. Jesus Christ, you know, my fondest wish is that we could do another one. But if we did, it would fuck everything up. It would just ruin everything.

Bums: You know, Walter is actually one of the most common costumes that we get at Lebowski Fests.

JG: Well, yeah, I bet there are a lot of fat guys out there. I don't even think I can get into my Walter vest anymore.

Bums: It's funny, though, we've had people come as giant severed toes—

JG: Yeah, I pretty much will not abide another toe.

Bums: We had a giant Creedence tape one year.

JG: [*laughing*] Yeah, I always wondered how the Eagles did out there.

Bums: We actually had a group come as the fucking Eagles last year, where they had eagle stuffed animals strapped to their underwear.

JG: [*laughing*] Jackie Treehorn draws a lot of water in Malibu, and you don't draw shit. I remember that fucking coffee cup. Perfect. Ever thus to deadbeats, Lebowski.

Bums: Not on the rug, man.

JG: Woo, I think we got the wrong guy.

Bums: Do you think Walter would have really pulled the trigger on Smokey?

JG: No . . . no . . . Well, you know what? I don't know. I think he would have had to, to make a point. I mean, at least put one in the leg.

Bums: This is not Nam. There are rules.

JG: Hey, come on, man, it's Smokey . . .

Bums: Have you seen the Comedy Central version of *The Big Lebowski?*

JG: It's hard to watch. It just grates on my ass because we went into the loop, and Joel and Ethan said, "You know, it's not going to match anyway, so say whatever you want."

Bums: So are you responsible for the line, "So you see what happens when you find a stranger in the Alps?"

JG: Yeah. Well, that actually might be Ethan. That sounds like Ethan, but, you know, we'd say anything. They didn't care. They knew it was going to be bogus anyway, so you might as well say the first thing that pops into your skull.

"What happens when you find a stranger in the Alps"

With almost three hundred F-bombs, The Big Lebowski is a challenge for any network to air. Here are the best of the TV-version overdubs as overheard by our brother shamuses on the LebowskiFest.com forum. Some of the contributions made by forum members were so good that we felt they should have been included in the TV version, even if they weren't.

Original line: They peed on my fucking rug.
TV version: They peed on my valued rug.

Original line: I don't need your fucking sympathy, man, I need my fucking johnson!

TV version: I don't need your sympathy, man, I need my penis!

Original line: Am I the only one around here who gives a shit about the rules?

TV version: Am I the only one around here who gives a stick about the rules?

Original line: I'll suck your cock for a thousand dollars.

TV version: I'll slurp your Coke for a thousand dollars.

Original line: If you don't like my fucking music, get your own fucking cab! . . . Outta my fucking cab!

TV version: If you don't like my peaceful music, get your own cab! . . . Outta my peaceful cab!

Original line: This is what happens when you fuck a stranger in the ass!

TV version: This is what happens when you find a stranger in the Alps and feed him scrambled eggs!

Original line: Tomorrow we come back and we cut off your johnson!

TV version: Tomorrow we come back and we cut off your toes!

Original line: I would've fucked you in the ass Saturday, I'll fuck you in the ass next Wednesday instead!

TV version: I would've met you in class on Saturday. I'll meet you in class next Wednesday instead!

Original line: Are you ready to be fucked, man?

TV version: Are you ready to be plucked, man?

Original line: Let me tell you something, *pendejo*. You pull any of your crazy shit with us, you flash a piece out on the lanes—I'll take it away from you and stick it up your ass and pull the fucking trigger till it goes click.

TV version: Let me tell you something, you crazy freak. If you try to pull any of your crazy stuff with us, you flash a piece out on the lanes, I'll take it away from you and stick it in your ear and pull the freaking trigger till it goes click.

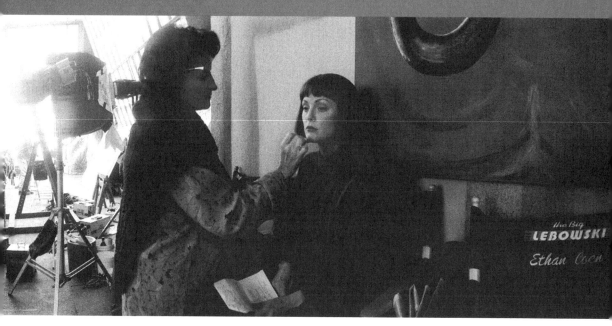

JULIANNE MOORE

Name: Julianne Moore

Character: Maude Lebowski

Born: Fayetteville, North Carolina, December 3, 1960

Select Filmography: *Children of Men, Hannibal, Magnolia, Boogie Nights, The Lost World: Jurassic Park, The Fugitive, Benny and Joon*

Trivia: Julianne debuted on the big screen in 1990 in *Tales from the Darkside: The Movie* as the victim of a mummy.

Bums: Can you tell us a little bit about how you got involved with the movie?

Julianne Moore: I was excited to be working with them, and I really liked the part. I thought it was super funny. The only thing I was worried about was that I had this idea about how she would speak, how it would sound, from how it was written. And I remember Ethan saying, "Yeah, I like that boarding school thing you have going on there." You know, it was really important to me how she would speak. Everyone says to me, "Well, where is Maude from?" And my response is, "She doesn't have an *accent*. She has an *affectation.*" There's a difference. She is really *tremendously* affected—which is what I loved about her. She's so pretentious she's almost beyond pretentious.

Bums: What was it like to work with the Coen brothers?

JM: *They are great.* So much of what they have to say to you is communicated in their language. In the way they write. And they are so specific in their writing. So much so that on one occasion I did one whole take, and Joel said, "That was great," and then Ethan came up to me and said, "Now do it again, but without the *really.*" And it was a speech that was a page long, and he wanted me to change this one word. But that's how specific he is.

Bums: A lot of people talk about *The Big Lebowski* as a buddy movie, a movie for the boys. But Maude is kind of the only real strong female presence in the film. She's articulate, she's strong-minded, she's an artist. Do you ever get any kind of response from other women about the film?

JM: [*flatly*] No. Just the men [*laughs*]. What I like about it is that there's nothing unequal— I mean, in a sense, there is inequality in the relationship between the Dude and Maude . . . because she's got all the power [*laughter*].

So what I like about it is that their way of communicating is tremendously direct. It's very balanced. The Dude respects Maude for what she is and what she does, and at the end of the day, Maude really respects the Dude. They both relate to each other in this very direct way. A real honest way.

> ## She's so pretentious she's almost beyond pretentious.

Bums: Yeah, the chemistry is there. What was it like working with Jeff Bridges?

JM: He's phenomenal. I'm *really* good at not laughing, and he might be the only actor I've ever worked with where it was actively difficult for me not to laugh. I really couldn't look at him. I really could not look at him. Especially when he said, "You mean, 'vagina'?" Unbelievable.

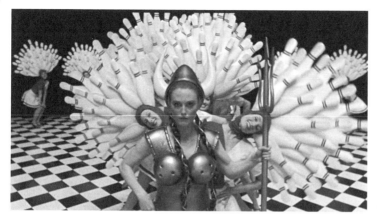

Bums: What was that like to film the dream sequence with all the choreography?

JM: It was hard. I was also pregnant. And I was *really* nauseous, and everything I did was incredibly difficult. It was *fun*, but I think Fran [Frances McDormand, married to Joel Coen] had just won her Academy Award—it was that morning, the day we were shooting. She literally won it the night before.

Bums: Did you have any idea why they were making you dress up like a valkyrie? It works so well, but why a valkyrie?

JM: Because it's the Dude's dream, man! That's what the Dude was dreaming! What I like about it is that it's so strangely powerful and romantic, from the Dude's perspective.

Bums: Do you have a favorite scene or a favorite line from the movie?

JM: My favorite line in the movie is actually Tara Reid's line when she says, "I'll suck your cock for a thousand dollars." That's my favorite.

Bums: Do you remember how you became aware that it began to gain this cult status?

JM: Mostly it was college students in the street saying, "Oh, I love *The Big Lebowski*, man." So it was usually kids who were in school and were up late. And then I started hearing about these conventions, and I said, "Are you kidding?"

Bums: It's a good time. Do you have any theories on what it is about this movie that resonates so strongly with people?

JM: Well, it's funny. It's really, really funny. I feel like we all kind of know people like the Dude, or have known people like the Dude in our lives, this whole idea that the Dude abides. He's always there, always doing his thing. There is something about him that is straightforward and honest, and he is who he is. And he's hung on to that, you know? He hasn't been deterred by time changing.

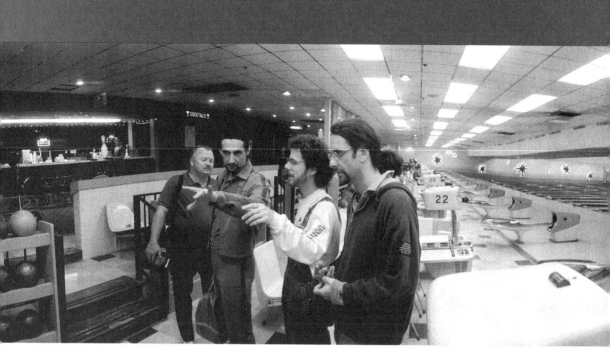

JOHN TURTURRO

Name: John Turturro

Character: Jesus Quintana aka the Jesus

Born: Brooklyn, February 28, 1957

Select Filmography: *The Good Shepherd*; *O Brother, Where Art Thou?*; *Box of Moonlight*; *Quiz Show*; *Barton Fink*; *Miller's Crossing*; *Do the Right Thing*

Trivia: Along with being a regular in Coen brothers films, John has also appeared in several films by Spike Lee.

John Turturro: Joel and Ethan, I've been talking to them about doing not exactly a sequel, but a spinoff of the Jesus. I wanna call it *The Second Coming*. I've got a whole scenario now and I'm going to meet with them and talk to them about it. I don't know if they would want to direct it, but maybe they would just write it. Low budget. The Jesus gets out of prison and you see him, and then he has to go to his brother and get a job. And he tries different jobs, and he winds up driving a school bus.

And then there is a sports team, and they usually have their own driver, but he replaces him, and he has to drive a school team of girl volleyball players. So it's kind of a road movie.

So you would see his trailer-trash father when he got out of prison. The guy lives in a trailer, and that would be like F. Murray Abraham. He'd be Joseph.

Then, like *The Bad News Bears*, he gets lured back into bowling. Or he tries to bowl and not be aggressive, but he's no good that way. He gets back in shape like Rocky. And then enters this big tournament and maybe wins money so that they can have a new volleyball field. Some shit like that.

And, you know, he prays for strength. And of course God is the Dude.

Bums: Of course.

JT: And the Dude comes and gives him, "Be cool. Hang out." So it's kind of like a spin-off. *The Second Coming*. He shows them all because he's an expert dancer of Latin dances. And maybe he hooks up with his old partner.

Bums: Liam!

JT: Liam. And the Jesus.

I always thought it was going to be a really big role, and when I first saw the script, I thought, Oh, there's not a lot here. But they knew I would come up with a lot of that physical stuff. They let me come up with a lot of my own ideas.

Now I love the movie. When I first saw it, I didn't completely get it. I think Jeff is sensational. I see all these guys winning Academy Awards for playing handicapped people, and the Dude is handicapped, too, you know [*laughs*]?

Bums: Yeah, it's amazing how little screen time you have, but how much resonance your character has. At the Lebowski Fests, that's always one of the more popular costumes.

JT: Yeah, well, it's a great costume. Joel and Ethan—that was their idea. My idea was the nail.

Bums: The coke nail was a slam dunk.

JT: When I go from door to door and knock on the door, they built me a huge codpiece and I didn't really want to wear it—I didn't wear it in the jumpsuit because it would have been

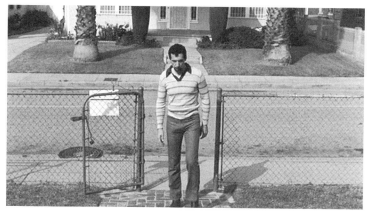

too much. There were cars that were literally *stopped* as I went from my trailer onto the set.

They let me come up with all of these crazy ideas like shining the ball. They say that's one of the most horrifying shots in all of their films. I figured, everyone in the film *talks* about the Jesus, so you gotta give them something to talk about. But every single thing I did, they put in.

The first time they showed it to me, when they were doing the mix, I put my head down. I was laughing, but I was really embarrassed. I thought, "I'm either going to be remembered forever or I'm ruined." But for those kind of guys, you do that.

I still get sex mail from that movie from all over the country.

Bums: Wow. How many times did you have to lick that ball?

JT: Not that many.

People have asked me on other movies, "Could you do something like you did in *The Big Lebowski?*" These are people who have no imagination. And I tell them, "You know what? I'm going to go back to my trailer, and you go back to your trailer. And you better think of something original to say to me." Screw that, you know what I mean? That's only for *those* guys.

Bums: What is it about the movie that gets to people so much?

JT: You know, seeing it again, I think they really captured that whole California mentality. But it's like a Cheech and Chong movie through the brains of Joel and Ethan. I think they just hit a vein with it.

Actually, what's very funny was to see Joel and Ethan imitate the Jesus for me before I did it. They would imitate for me: "I take that gun and stick it up your ass and go *click*!" Over and over again. And to see them both do it was *hilarious*.

> # I'm either going to be remembered forever or I'm ruined.

Bums: People say that scene where you're dancing in slow motion is some of the best film footage in cinematic history.

JT: My idea for that was Muhammad Ali, that dance backwards. I did it and they loved that. When I showed them that shining thing, they fell down laughing. They were thinking maybe the Jesus really only has one ball. But it's giant.

Joel and Ethan's mom, when she was alive, would say, *"I don't know how the boys come up with these things!"* Well, they're obviously very secure with who they are.

Bums: One more question, on the topic of a sequel. John Goodman mentioned *The Second Coming,* and said that the Coen brothers say they're only going to do one sequel and it's called *Old Fink.* They're going to wait until you get older and do a sequel to *Barton Fink.*

JT: Yeah, *that* they're serious about. This, I just wanted them to write. They don't have to direct this. I'll direct it myself. I'll make a low-budget film of the Jesus. I feel like I have to do it for *The Big Lebowski* fans. Almost like I have no choice now. And I've got to do it within the next couple of years.

I tell them, "We can make like the lowest-budget film of all time. It's about the *Jesus.*" It's not a sequel. *Old Fink* is a sequel. This is more of a spin-off. Starring, you know, the Jesus.

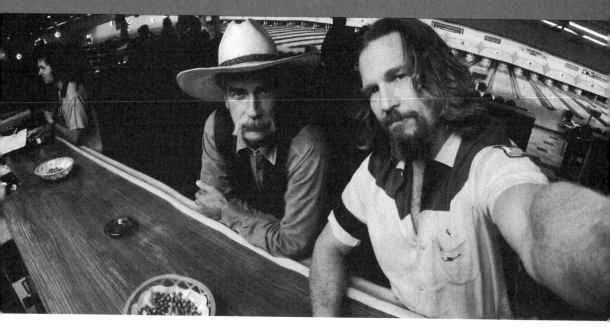

SAM ELLIOTT

Name: Sam Elliott

Character: The Stranger

Born: Sacramento, California, August 9, 1944

Select Filmography: *Thank You for Smoking*, *Off the Map*, *The Contender*, *Tombstone*, *Gettysburg*, *Road House*, *Mask*

Trivia: Sam made his big-screen debut in *Butch Cassidy and the Sundance Kid* and later married Katharine Ross, who played the film's female lead.

Bums: First, how did you come to be involved in the project?

Sam Elliott: Years earlier, I had heard from a guy named Jim Jacks, who I believe produced *Raising Arizona*, and he said, "You know, the Coen brothers are big fans of yours." We're sitting there around the pool one day in Tucson, Arizona. So I said, "Oh, cool." And he said, "No, really. They'd love to work with you one day." So I kinda flushed that shit out of my head. We all want to believe, but how rarely does it happen?

So I'm down in Texas and here comes this script. And not only is it the Coen brothers,

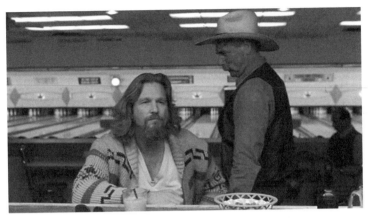

but it's got my name in it! The interesting thing was that they spelled my fucking name wrong! It didn't matter. It was an opportunity to work with people that I have a lot of respect for as filmmakers. It was a chance to work with somebody who I consider a contemporary of mine, and I've watched his career from day one. He's the guy who gets all the shit that I'd love to have done some of over the years—that's Bridges.

Bums: Did you ever think about why the character of the Stranger was in the movie, or did the Coens ever talk to you about that? About what purpose he served?

SE: You know, I think you can kind of intellectualize and psychoanalyze this shit to death probably. But that's not my m.o. I'm doing well to get the lines down and hit the fucking marks. In terms of why he was there, you'd have to ask the brothers about that. He was some voice of reason, I feel. Some sort of conscience, for lack of a better way to put it.

> ## Just drifting along, man. The wind caught him.

Just take for example the fact that he was put off by the foulmouthed shit. Obviously I'm not. But as a character, he's put off by it. And I think that that spoke for probably a lot of people that watched that movie because there was so much of that kind of dialogue in it.

Bums: What was it like to shoot that final summing-up speech?

SE: Well, I was only there on the set two days, and I never got out of the fucking bowling alley, did I? I just went from one end of the room to the other. That was it. So I'm sitting there doing the scene at the bar, and fuck, it's going on forever! I did more takes of that scene than anything I've ever done in my career.

Finally I looked at Joel—Joel's on one side and Ethan's on the other—and said, "What the fuck is up here? Or what isn't up? I mean, what's going on? You gotta tell me what you want." And they both say, in unison, "Aw, fuck, we got it on take eight. We just like seeing you do it."

Bums: One more question about that scene. You may not remember this, but after you finish your speech you get up and walk in one direction and then—

SE: I turn around and go the other way!

Bums: Yeah! Was that scripted or was that spontaneous?

SE: Well, it was kind of both. It wasn't scripted, but I got up and I started to go out one way and I said, "What way do you want me to go?" And I think Joel said, "Fuck, I don't know man, go both ways!"

I think the false start came initially from me, and they saw it and they said, "Oh yeah, that's cool! He doesn't know where the fuck he's going."

Bums: You're just drifting along.

SE: Just drifting along, man. The wind caught him.

Jeff and I went through that whole thing where we're sitting at the fucking bar wondering if the Stranger was coming up and hitting on him. Kind of looking at the cowboy gear and all that shit and thinking, "Well, what the fuck is this guy about?" That was our little movie going on. It was a lot of fun.

That's a good one. Sarsaparilla is a vine that bears roots that can be used to flavor beverages such as root beer. Sioux City sarsaparilla is manufactured by the White Rock Beverage Company and was first introduced in 1975. At that time it came in a twelve-ounce steel can with innovative action graphics. In 1986 it was changed to the current, embossed brown bottle and achieved national distribution. Sioux City sarsaparilla was the first beverage to capture the flavor of the Old West and is known as the leader of all sarsaparilla drinks.

Bums: There's the line that you say, that famous line, "Sometimes you eat the bar, and sometimes he eats you." Are you saying "bear" or "bar"?

SE: No, I'm saying "bar." But it's bar in that sense, you know, in the sense of bear. It's not the bar on which we're leaning. But that was the Coens, that's the way they wrote it, you know? Sometimes you eat the bar and sometimes, well, sometimes he eats you.

You guys are all way too young, but there was this series on TV called *Daniel Boone*. A guy named Fess Parker was the star of it, based on this historical character but a total Hollywood treatment of him. This guy was purported to be a guy who had killed a couple of bears with his bare hands, with a blade. And he was always talking about bears, but he always called them "bars." They're gonna getcha! I don't know where the fuck they got it.

But I think that on some level, every character—I mean, look at Jesus—he's so over the line. I think that's true of the Stranger, too, on some levels. He was cool—I don't mean that—but he was . . . He had a big white hat on.

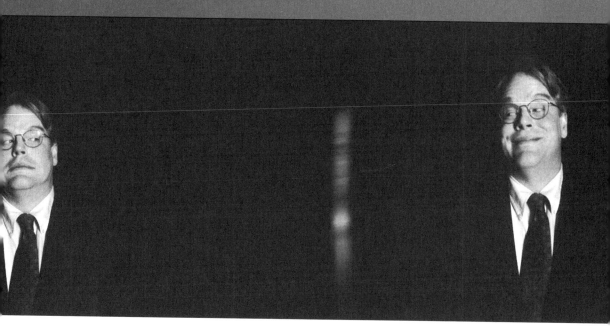

PHILIP SEYMOUR HOFFMAN

Name: Philip Seymour Hoffman

Character: Brandt

Born: Rochester, New York, July 23, 1967

Select Filmography: *Capote, Owning Mahowny, 25th Hour, Punch-Drunk Love, Love Liza, Almost Famous, The Talented Mr. Ripley*

Trivia: Philip has acted in three movies with Julianne Moore—*Magnolia, The Big Lebowski,* and *Boogie Nights.*

Bums: How did you first meet the Coens?

Philip Seymour Hoffman: I think it was at the audition. I had to prepare a couple of scenes. I remember doing the scene where I'm showing the Dude around the office and they were laughing a lot. I remember thinking I made them laugh. I didn't know if I would get the job, but I felt good that I made them laugh because I was a big fan of the Coen brothers' films. *Raising Arizona* is hilarious.

Bums: How did they describe the character of Brandt to you?

PSH: They didn't really talk a lot about that. There was some person it was loosely based on, but not really. They wouldn't dictate to me. They backed off and let me be. I was making pretty strong choices about the character.

Bums: One thing that people always mention when they talk about Brandt is the repeated dialogue, especially where you say "the necessary means" twice in a row. How did that come about?

PSH: Well, I think it was originally written as if he were having a new thought. I think it was written as if he would say, "the necessary means," and then say it again but in a new way. And I just did it where he repeats himself.

> # I didn't feel the need to be natural or realistic.

I think it came from some aspect that he has, a way of presenting things that he's done so many times before in the same way. So out of fear, or anxiety and a need to please, he just kind of regurgitates it [*laughing*]. It just falls out of his mouth in a way where he has no ownership of it whatsoever. That's why the "Yes, yes." His need to please his boss and whatever that means is so out of hand that he just has become this kind of person.

Bums: Yeah, that scene gets us every time. Brandt could have easily come across as kind of a caricature, but you were able to avoid that. Were you worried about that with the role?

PSH: Not really, because I think the film is a pretty stylized film—it's not a naturalistic film to me. The film is a little bit on another plane. So the characters are allowed to be bigger than life. I didn't feel the need to be natural or realistic.

Bums: In addition to the dialogue, part of what makes the character of Brandt so great are his physical mannerisms, little things like where you'll shrug your shoulders or wince. How did those come about?

PSH: Those are the kinds of things that came out of what I was working on. They would say how it's as if you're trying to hold yourself together—the anxiety that he had that everything needed to go well. And when the Dude was around, everything ended up going to shit.

Bums: Do you have any thoughts on why this movie resonates so strongly with certain people?

PSH: I remember the first time I watched it—and probably the last time I watched it and every other time—but I remember when the Stranger, Sam Elliott, at the end, says, "The Dude abides." [*with a Sam Elliott impression*] "The Dude abides." And I think that's why it does, because I think everybody wishes that that's what life was like.

If everyone treated each other in such a way. "I'll abide by you and you abide by me, and we'll be just fine." And there is something beautiful in that. And that's what's great about Coen brothers movies in general, I think: There's always a certain something that's being said there, in a very humble way. That to me is why.

But it's also the first hour of the film is just hysterical, and then you get to the end and you realize there is really something about this film that people wish that's how everyone lived, you know? That we all abided by each other. But they do it in a way that makes you laugh. The Stranger—doesn't he go for the peanuts or something?

Bums: Yeah, and then he walks off one way and kind of turns around and goes back the other way. We asked Sam Elliott about that and he said, "The wind took me." Do you have a

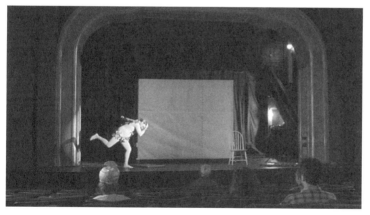

favorite character or a favorite scene or a favorite line?

PSH: I like that line a lot, I think it's a really groovy moment. I have to say I think my favorite thing is Kehler when he comes for the rent. And then he goes to this performance piece—the dance thing he does?

Bums: The cycle.

PSH: That's fuckin' too much. And then the opening sequence where he's drinking the milk out of the carton is hysterical. Really great. There's tons of funny shit in it, but Kehler when he has to go to the show and they're all talking about what they're going to do, and he's dancing up there . . .

Bums: And there's like five people in the audience.

PSH: And doesn't Goodman tell him to shut up or something?

Bums: Yeah, he yells at Donny. "Shut the fuck up, Donny!" And Bridges says, "Shhh!" Dude's trying to make him be quiet.

PSH: That's good. Really good.

Bums: Do people ever recognize you as Brandt anymore, now that you're so well known for other roles?

PSH: Not as much anymore as a few years ago—it used to be a lot more—but you find out the hard-core *Lebowski* fans. They just yell, "Brandt!" and you know they're hard-core.

Bums: Are there any specific lines they always say?

PSH: The way I repeat the lines is the thing they mention most. And also the stuff with Bunny. But usually they just yell, "Brandt!"

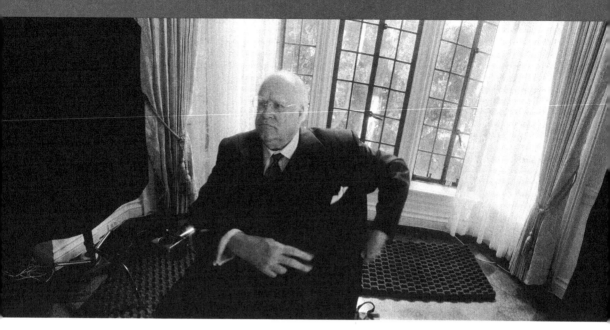

DAVID HUDDLESTON

Name: David Huddleston

Character: The Big Lebowski

Born: Vinton, Virgina, September 17, 1930

Select Filmography: *The Producers, Joe's Apartment, Santa Claus, Blazing Saddles, Bad Company*

Trivia: David's television appearances include *Bewitched, Bonanza, Gunsmoke, The Rockford Files, Hawaii Five-O, Sanford and Son, Charlie's Angels,* and *The West Wing,* among many others.

Bums: One thing we were interested in is how the Coen brothers discovered you. We've heard that they saw you act in a play. Is that true?

David Huddleston: I went in on a regular audition and then, God! There were so many well-known faces. Finally it came my turn to go in, and first thing one of them said, "Didn't I see you in *Death of a Salesman* with Dustin Hoffman?"

Then, later on, before we started shooting, after we had gotten cast, everybody came in and sat around at a table and read it. We did kind of a prerehearsal, and that was very valuable to me. Because you see who you're working with.

I had done a picture with Jeff Bridges in the early seventies, so we were good friends. Sam Elliott is a close friend. So it was good being there with all those guys.

Bums: It's hard to imagine anyone playing the Big Lebowski but you. Did you just slide right in to the character?

DH: No, that's not how I work. These fellas—they both direct at the same time. In fact, they both do everything at the same time, and they are hands-on from the first minute to the last minute.

They would tell me what they wanted in the scene, and we'd rehearse it, and they'd say, "We want it bigger," or "We want it littler." And we'd do it several times, and they'd get what they wanted. And sometimes—and this was really good for the actor, I've never had this happen before—sometimes they would say, "Okay, we've got what *we* want. Is there anything you want to do?" And they would give you that option, which was good. I liked it.

Bums: Can you remember any particular scene where they gave you that option?

DH: That scene in the car where I say, "I will not abide another toe." We did it over and over and over again. You know, they write the way you talk, and if you try to *act* their writing, it doesn't work. For me, anyway. You just have to learn it syllable by syllable and comma by comma, and it comes out okay. The "ahs," the "ers," the "Oh, my God!" or whatever.

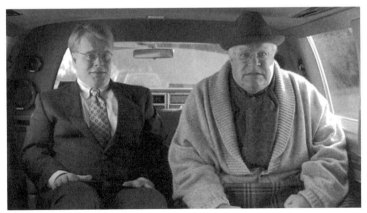

Bums: Yeah, that little speech that Jeff Bridges gives in the limo is quite intense, and that was all scripted exactly like that, right? All the "ums" and "uhs" and "sirs" were written exactly the way it's filmed?

DH: Exactly.

Bums: But Bridges makes it seem so natural.

DH: That's why he gets big bucks.

Bums: Looking over the list of roles you've done in your career, it's pretty amazing. There are more than 130 listings, and there are probably even more than that for items that aren't here, stage plays and whatnot. What do you think you are best known for at this point?

DH: I think it would probably be *The Big Lebowski*. I have been so lucky to be in pictures like this. When I did *Blazing Saddles*, it was just a bomb. It didn't make that much money. And it became kind of a cult picture, and now kids come up to me and recite every goddamn line that I had to say in the picture. They do the same thing with *Lebowski*.

Bums: Have you watched the movie many times?

DH: Oh, I've seen it several times. In fact, just last week I saw it. There are certain scenes that I really love. There is a scene where the Little Lebowski and John Goodman are sitting at a counter and having a cup of coffee, and they start arguing about something and getting loud, and the lady asks them to leave, and Lebowski leaves, and there's a moment where John says, "I'm staying." "I'm staying here, enjoying my coffee. Enjoying my coffee." I love that scene. "Enjoying my coffee."

And I love the scene, "Nobody fucks with the Jesus!"

Bums: John Turturro.

DH: Yeah, yeah. Don't fuck with Jesus!

Bums: What did you think when Philip Seymour Hoffman won the Oscar?

DH: I was very proud. He's a wonderful actor, and he and I got along very, very well in the picture. At least to me, he was not totally unknown but almost unknown at that point. He had done *Boogie Nights* before that, but I thought he was a nice guy, and he is a terrific actor. As a matter of fact, I'm a member of the Academy, and I certainly voted for him to win it.

The one thing that bothers me is that we did the picture, and it's done very well and become a cult classic, and I thought I did pretty good in it. And these guys have never called me again. For any of their pictures.

They made that Southern one, *O Brother, Where Art Thou?* and there was a damn good part in there for me! But they haven't seen fit to do that, I don't know why.

Bums: If they happen to grant us an interview, we'll ask them.

DH: Just say, "The Big Lebowski wants to know why you hate him" [*laughs*].

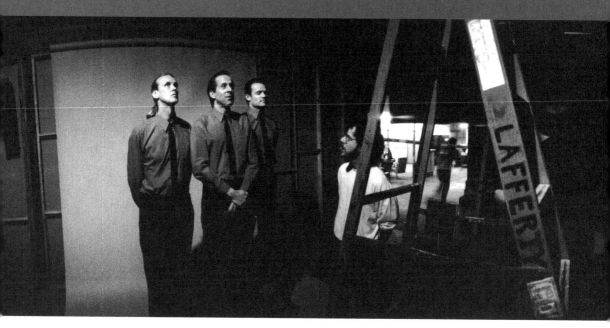

PETER STORMARE

Name: Peter Stormare

Character: Nihilist #1, Uli Kunkel, Karl Hungus

Born: Arbra, Sweden, August 27, 1953

Select Filmography: *Nacho Libre, Constantine, Minority Report, Chocolat, Dancer in the Dark, 8MM, Armageddon, Fargo*

Trivia: Peter and his band, Blonde from Fargo, performed at a Lebowski Fest in Los Angeles.

Bums: How did you develop the character of Uli?

Peter Stormare: It started as a spoof between Ethan and I on the set of *Fargo*. I'd speak in that mock German accent. [*in German accent*] *"I'm a very evil, evil doctor. Now don't touch this button because the whole world vill disappear!"*

Bums: In *Fargo*, your character constantly wants to go to "Pancakes House," and then in *Lebowski* you get to have some pigs in a blanket and pancakes. Are those related?

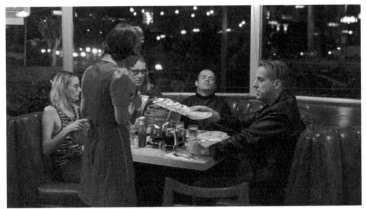

PS: I'm sure! They have an obsession with pancakes. It's a Midwestern thing, I guess. I had never had pancakes. I grew up in Sweden, and I'm not a big fan of pancakes.

A funny thing happened while we were filming *Fargo*. It was like five o'clock in the morning after shooting all night, and the Coen brothers had arranged for us to go to this legendary pancakes house in Minneapolis. Steve Buscemi was driving. Steve Buscemi is a tremendous actor, but he's not a very good driver!

So it's the middle of the night, it's dark, it's February in Minneapolis, and as he was driving he went the wrong way down a one-way street. Luckily there was no one out and we cut over and made a left into this place and parked the car.

Immediately we were hit by a light and we heard this big megaphone: "Please remain in the car!" I'd already started to get out and the voice said, "Sir, get back into the car!" I thought it was the Coen brothers joking with us, and I was like, "Yeah, yeah." But the voice came again: "Step into the car!" All of a sudden a female cop came out with a fucking gun! I was quick to get into the car. She walked up and said, "What the hell are you doing, guys?"

And Steve Buscemi tried to flirt! It was exactly like the scene in *Fargo*. It's so bizarre. So he was trying to flirt and said, "We're shooting a movie up here. We're actors from New York." But she wasn't interested. She said, "I've been working for two days straight." The cop asked for his registration and driver's license, and he pulled it out and looked at me and rolled his eyes.

Then she said, "What is this, sir?" It was the exact same line as in the movie. We weren't sure if this was a setup or not, but she was pretty scary, this woman and her gun. And Steve had actually taken out his Mastercard instead of his driver's license! Then she said, "I'm not going to ticket you, but you're a guest of this city and you should abide the law. You shouldn't be driving around like this."

When we finally got to the pancake house, everybody was there. We told them the story, but they didn't believe us. It could have totally been set up by them as a practical joke.

Bums: So do you think it was the Coen brothers that set that up?

PS: I'm really not sure!

Bums: How did you first meet the Coen brothers?

PS: I was working back in Sweden doing *Hamlet*. We were touring and did a festival in New York, and Ethan sat together with one of the casting people. They invited me to come by their editing room, where they were editing *Raising Arizona*. While I was there they said they had a certain script in mind and they may have a little part for me in *Miller's Crossing*. A part they called the Swede, this crazy guy, a sniper running on the rooftops shooting people. But I couldn't do it because I couldn't get a sabbatical from my theater. If it would have only been a few months later, it would have been a dream come true. To make a long story short, I didn't end up in *Miller's Crossing*, and they renamed the character the Dane.

Bums: What's the difference between Joel and Ethan?

PS: [*laughs*] Ethan is a walker and Joel is the talker. Both can walk and both can talk. If there is a scene, Ethan always walks away to leave Joel to do the directing. He watches the replay and then goes and talks to Joel. Joel nods his head, and then Ethan comes over and says, "Maybe you should try to inhale before you say, 'come on'—like a deep inhale." Lots of things like that, and I'm always left feeling like, "Where the fuck did he get that from?" They are very, very specific. Contrary to most directors, you can actually see their script up there on the screen. It's already edited in their heads. And it makes you feel comfortable because you can concentrate on being just an actor and you can really just play the part. So many directors, they don't do their homework.

With the Coens they know exactly: "You come here, you go there, lift your glass, now put it down . . ." They are very specific, and it makes you happy. You can just concentrate, like being a football player. You don't have to think about the logistics of the team, you just play football and do your best. You just act. You don't have to think about anything else.

You're only allowed to drown them twice, then you have to use a new ferret.

Bums: What was it like doing the *Log-jammin'* scene?

PS: I didn't know who Asia Carrera was. She said, "This is my name, this is my card, check me out on the Web." I looked her up, and man, she's plastered all over the place! I didn't know that she was a porn star. She was very, very smart. We had great conversations. If I had known before what she had done with her body I would have been a little intimidated.

Bums: Is that the only porn you've done?

PS: That's the only one I've done. I wouldn't mind being Karl Hungus in *Logjammin' 2* or number 69.

Bums: Why do people like this movie so much?

PS: It's like an homage to California. But at the same time, in my home country of Sweden they love *The Big Lebowski*, too, and in Germany and Italy—everywhere I've been. I didn't know that it was such a global thing.

It's a combination of the craziness of being a regular human being and ending up in such a mess. Everything's so bizarre. It's like California. I thought it would never take off in other parts of the U.S., but it definitely did, especially the DVD.

Bums: We've got to ask you about the marmot. Did the ferret have a name?

PS: [*laughs*] No. You could only use them like three or four times due to the regulations of the animal activists. You're only allowed to drown them twice, then you have to use a new ferret. I would have to take the ferret and give it over to the wrangler, who treats it real nice and gives it a hair blower and all that. The animals are treated better than the actors.

Bums: Do you have a favorite scene from the movie, or a favorite character?

PS: I don't watch movies of myself. I don't think I've ever seen *The Big Lebowski*. I've seen bits and pieces, and I love that scene with Steve Buscemi's burial and the Dude is up there by the ocean and the wind blows the ashes. I dig Sam Elliott in the beginning and how he closes the whole show. I'm glad he said yes to the film, because without him it wouldn't have been the same. It's a little bit mocking himself, but at the same time I think he's such a talented guy, he knew what it was all about. He did the movie a really big favor. He really ties it in beautifully. It becomes kind of a fairy tale. It has kind of a story-time feel to it. It's a legend.

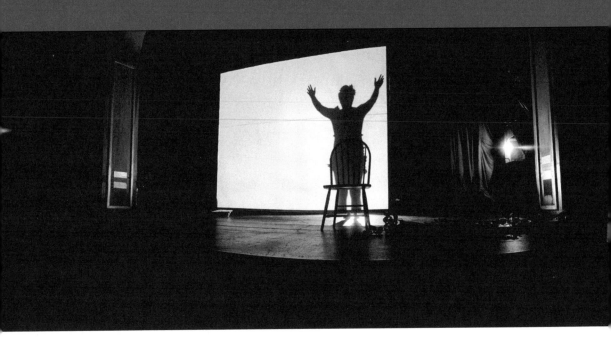

JACK KEHLER

Name: Jack Kehler

Character: Marty the Landlord

Born: Philadelphia, May 22, 1946

Select Filmography: *This Is Not a Film, Men in Black II, Love Liza, Austin Powers: The Spy Who Shagged Me, Lost Highway, Wyatt Earp, The Last Boy Scout, Point Break*

Trivia: Jack is not a dancer by trade.

Bums: People really enjoy Marty the Landlord. Do you have any insight on why such a small role has affected people so much?

Jack Kehler: It's funny, my wife and I just came back from Edinburgh, Scotland. We were walking down the street and this young guy came up to me and said, "I thought it was you! *The Big Lebowski*. Your character has influenced a lot of comedians over here in Britain!"

But you know, I don't have any idea other than I just seemed to be a regular guy doing my work. Collecting the rent. I got to talking with the guy from Edinburgh, and he said, "It just seemed like you inherited those apartments from your father, and you just had to keep doing your job. And it was something you really weren't comfortable with."

So it's somewhere in there: the discomfort of having to do something, and still having this separate secret life of dancing. Something about that reverberates with people.

Bums: There is something that's really sweet about the relationship between you, the landlord, and the Dude. It's like the landlord kind of looks up to him and wants to be his buddy. He doesn't want to ask for the rent, but he kind of has to.

JK: He had to! And it's so funny because even in the scene physically, I'm looking up to him. It's really true. And the Dude has found a peace with living in this world and found a way to do it. Not on the high end, not on the success end, and getting along. And that's attractive.

Bums: Yeah, he's cool enough to come to your dance quintet and give you notes, you know?

JK: How about that! But it's true, he really does. And I do come to ask him. I ask him to do that because I know that he'll appreciate it.

Bums: In the midst of all that stuff, he says, "I'll be there, man."

JK: *Yeah!*

Bums: So, that little fist pump that you do—did you improvise that?

JK: Yeah, I did that. I really got bummed because the dance quintet got cut off so quickly.

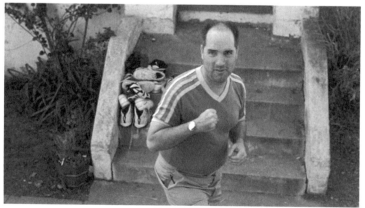

When the people applaud, I bow, and then I give the fist pump again. I was so bummed when I saw that. I said, "Oh, no, it's not in there!"

Bums: So can you tell us a little about the

> ## And I am *completely* . . . I'm *not* a dancer. I mean, you may not know that . . .

dance quintet? Where did you get those moves?

JK: Bill and Jacqui Landrum. They are a dance-choreographer team who did all the choreography for the movie. The Coens arranged three three-hour rehearsals at their dance studio. And I am *completely* . . . I'm *not* a dancer. I mean, you may not know that . . .

So the first time I went there, they said, "Okay, these are the choices of music that the brothers want us to listen to." And we listened to three or four pieces of classical music, and I chose one, *Pictures at an Exhibition.* So then they took me through each little phase of music and said, "Okay, now how does this make you feel?"

And I say this or that, and they would say, "Okay, show me physically."

And so the three rehearsals, that's what we did. We literally went bar by bar, and they made me express myself physically with that.

Burns: Do you remember any specific emotions that came to you when they said, "How does this make you feel?"

JK: Just the struggle. It feels like a struggle. Then there was a part when I'm bent over and I'm going sideways with my arm out, and on that one I feel like I am being challenged and I have to deal with it, with the force that is coming at me. And then I do. I overcome it and make my way up to the chair and something flows out of me. All the beauty . . .

They would say, "What do you feel now? Does that sound make you feel like someone is coming at you and you have to protect yourself?" And I'd say, "*Yes.* Yes, it does." It was a trip.

I was sorry that you didn't see the audience from my point of view, because there were about eight people in the audience interspersed all over the theater. And it's a huge theater. And then when it was over, you heard one guy clap a couple of times.

My God, did I get a giggle out of that.

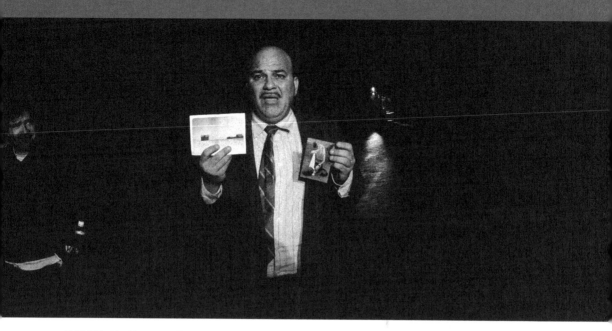

JON POLITO

Name: John Polito

Character: Da Fino (Private Snoop)

Born: Philadelphia, December 29, 1950

Select Filmography: *Flags of Our Fathers, The Man Who Wasn't There, The Adventures of Rocky and Bullwinkle, The Crow, The Hudsucker Proxy, Barton Fink, Miller's Crossing, The Freshman*

Trivia: John once performed as a woman on *The Chris Isaak Show*.

Bums: How did you meet the Coen brothers?

John Polito: The Coen brothers and I met back in '89. I read the script for *Miller's Crossing*, and I wanted very much to go in on the character of Johnny Caspar. But in fact the Coens didn't really see me as Johnny Caspar. They saw me as the Dane. But I didn't want to go be seen for anything else, because that script, and especially that first speech of Johnny Caspar, was like a piece of music. I was able to actually learn those lines after just reading the script about two or three times.

Bums: To our count, you've been in five Coen brothers films, and that makes you and Steve Buscemi the most Coened actors.

JP: Good! I'm glad to hear it. You know the thing about the Coens—when I was a kid I loved all the old movies. I remember when I first saw Orson Welles's films. It was a company of actors that he was working with over and over again, and I knew there was something that was different than the regular motion pictures. I really feel like the Coen brothers are like the Mercury Theater Company—that group that Welles had. Working for them is like working for the new Orson Welles.

Bums: Do you have a favorite role that you've played for the Coen brothers?

JP: Well, I have to tell you that they are all different. *Miller's Crossing* is definitely my favorite gangster role. But then again, in *The Man Who Wasn't There* I got to come out of the closet and make a pass at Billy Bob Thornton. I'll tell you, that Billy Bob is pretty cute.

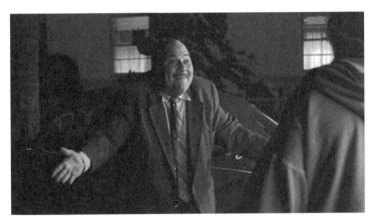

Bums: How many times are you going to get a chance like that?

JP: Not many, unfortunately, because he swings the other way. No variation in his sexuality.

Bums: Seeing as how they keep casting you over and over again, do you know what it is they like about you so much?

JP: I'm brilliant [*laughs*]. You know what it is about them, which is quite amazing: Whatever they saw in me, whatever they brought out of me, is part of their gift. Their vision is really what has made my career change. I would have been a regular, kind of solid actor, but I don't think I would have ever had great performances under my belt without the Coen brothers.

Bums: So we've got to get to *The Big Lebowski*.

JP: Yeah, which has turned out to be quite a cult film, I understand—for the dopers.

Bums: When did you begin to find out that *The Big Lebowski* was gaining a cult following?

JP: That happened much later. I don't think the movie opened to much acclaim, really. I thought it the most Salvador Dalíesque of their films on one hand, and on the other hand it was like a perfect American-international trip movie from the sixties.

I didn't really know how much it was catching on until one day someone walked up to me and said, "I'm a dick, man, just like you." I had no idea what they were talking about! Finally they would get to the part about, "You know, a brother shamus." And then I figured it out, and I began to realize that there were these festivals going on.

Bums: Do people ever come up and ask you why you're following them?

JP: Well, exactly. Even if I'm walking ahead of them. It's been a curse and a joy in my existence, in my theatrical existence, being part of a classic like *Lebowski*.

Bums: Would you say, "I'm a dick, just like you!" is the most common line you hear?

JP: I would say, "I'm a dick, just like you." I gotta tell you, that warms up the room when you enter.

Bums: Do you have a favorite character or line from the movie?

JP: You know what my favorite thing is? The Knudsens.

Bums: Who the fuck are the Knudsens?

JP: I mean, I like the whole thing working with Jeff in that scene there, but something about saying "Knudsens" just strikes me.

And you know, it's very difficult as an actor to walk in and play a one-scene character.

Because they didn't really need me for all the Volkswagen shots—they just had a Volkswagen behind with a driver.

So I walked into it rather cold. And because of the competition—coming out being afraid, but at the same time wanting to hold my own with Jeff Bridges, and he's a taller guy—I found I couldn't quite get the lines out where I felt confident enough. So I found myself punctuating the lines in my head by lifting up on my heels. I'm kind of standing up on my heels and I go up and down on these lines.

Bums: Yeah, it always cracks us up how he kind of raises his fist at you, how he kind of lifts his arms up like he's going to fight you.

JP: Well, the funny thing about that scene is it's a battle between two really wussy guys. We know how to pose like we're battling, but who's gonna throw the first punch there?

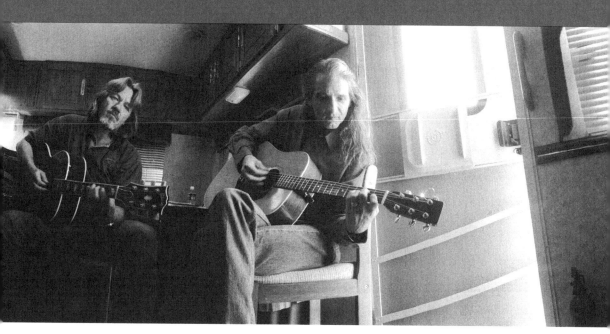

JIMMIE DALE GILMORE

Name: Jimmie Dale Gilmore

Character: Smokey

Born: Lubbock, Texas, May 6, 1945

Select Filmography: Appeared performing in a honky-tonk in *Monster's Ball* and had a cameo in Peter Bogdanovich's *The Thing Called Love*. He also wrote and performed songs in the film.

Trivia: Jimmie Dale is a practicing Buddhist and, like Smokey, a pacifist.

Bums: First, we have an unrelated question. What was the first concert you ever attended?

Jimmie Dale Gilmore: I can't tell you the first, because my dad took me to a lot of gigs—he was a country-western fan and also was a player himself. But the first one that I really remember clearly was Elvis Presley and Johnny Cash.

I tell people that was most likely the night that sealed the deal that I would be a musician. I've also heard that it's the show that Buddy Holly was at that turned him around and turned him in the rock 'n' roll direction.

Bums: Can you tell us about how you came to be a part of *The Big Lebowski?*

JDG: I don't know the specifics, but Joel and Ethan had been coming to gigs, and they actually had talked to me on a couple of occasions about the possibility of doing some music. So when they called and asked me to play a part, I was completely shocked because I'm not an actor. That's not my role. But they told me not to worry. They said they would babysit me—which they did.

It wasn't until I read the script later that I knew anything about what it was about. And I didn't really have to know anything, because I love the Coen brothers—they've been my favorite filmmakers for a long time. And still remain that way. I think some of the Coen brothers stuff is as good as the old slapstick. And that's about the highest compliment I can pay to a moviemaker!

Bums: In terms of the character of Smokey, he's a pacifist in the film, and we've read that you're a practicing Buddhist. Could you relate at all to Smokey on a personal level?

JDG: I really have the sense that that probably is the way I might react to an actual situation like that. Although I also kind of think that just about anybody would!

John Goodman is, both as Walter and as John, a totally towering presence. Very, very powerful. And even though it's acting, he's really got that vibe. He can go from being so sweet, bighearted, and loving a person . . . but he can be scary!

Bums: It's cool that the Coens were fans of your music before you were cast in their film. Aimee Mann is also in the movie, and Flea is in the movie. We don't know if you noticed it, but you get a gun pulled on you, Aimee Mann has a toe cut off, and Flea has a bowling ball thrown in his stomach.

JDG: I never thought of that!

Bums: Do the Coen brothers have some sort of animosity towards musicians?

JDG: Well, not in my experience!

Bums: But they definitely have some hostility towards the Eagles!

JDG: That's one of the signature scenes in the movie to me. The whole sequence where the Dude is with the sheriff, and then gets a ride with the cab driver who gets mad because he hates the Eagles. That is so hilarious.

Bums: So do you have any idea what it is about the movie that appeals to people so much?

JDG: Well, I've had several friends who were somehow similar to the Dude. Very, very laid-back guys. Highly intelligent people who had opted out of the rat race mentality. And I think that's a lot of it.

And there's more than that—it's because of a friendship between these opposite personalities. The personality of Walter and of the Dude, those guys are so utterly different. But in real life that happens a lot! Good friends who are entirely different from each other.

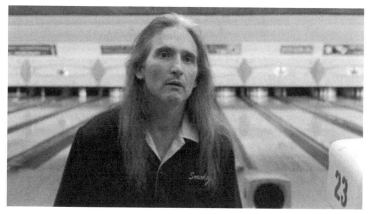

Bums: How did you first start to realize that it was becoming a cult hit? How did you start to hear about the following?

JDG: Well, first of all, I started noticing that—particularly if I was around college campuses in my touring and stuff—more and more often people started coming up to me and saying, "Are you Smokey?" And now it's constant.

Or sometimes they'll ask me, "Were you over the line?" Like they think it really happened, and I'm the only one that knows it!

Bums: What do you tell them when they ask you that?

JDG: I say, "Oh, no, not me!"

And it's an odd thing: most of the people who know me from the movie don't even know that I am a musician. I told Joel and Fran that I've been playing music professionally for getting close to forty years, and I've gotten more attention for two minutes in a Coen brothers movie than for forty years of playing music!

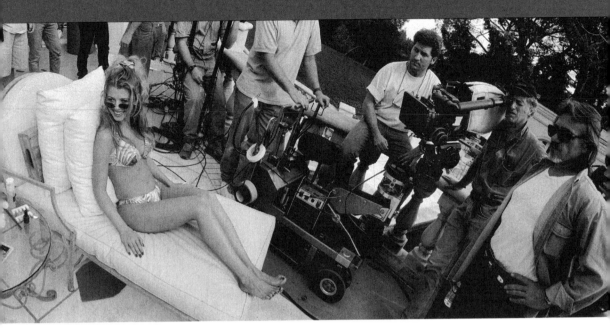

TARA REID

Name: Tara Reid

Character: Bunny Lebowski, Bunny La Joya, Fawn Knudsen

Born: Wyckoff, New Jersey, November 8, 1975

Select Filmography: *Van Wilder, Josie and the Pussycats, American Pie, Cruel Intentions*

Trivia: Tara still has all ten of her toes.

Bums: How did you become involved with *The Big Lebowski*? What was your audition like?

Tara Reid: I auditioned for it and then went back for the callback. I was in the room with Charlize Theron, among others. I thought to myself, For sure I am not getting this role. Then I got the call from my agent saying I got the part!

Bums: You deliver one of the best lines of the movie [the thousand-dollar one]. Did you nail that on the first take, or did it take several?

TR: We shot four different angles, and the director picked the best one.

> **The cable did not get fixed. He was a little too busy fixing other things.**

Bums: Did you ever find it hard to keep a straight face anywhere else?

TR: It was very hard to keep a straight face on set; we had a blast.

Bums: What was your family's reaction to your role in the film?

TR: They loved it and thought it was a great movie.

Bums: We loved you in *Logjammin'*. Did the cable ever get fixed?

TR: No, the cable did not get fixed. He was a little too busy fixing other things.

Bums: Do people ever recognize you as Bunny Lebowski? What do they usually say to you?

TR: All the time. People love Bunny, and they say I had the best lines in the movie.

Bums: How did being in *The Big Lebowski* change your career?

TR: *The Big Lebowski* opened doors to new opportunities that I did not have before, and it took me to the next level.

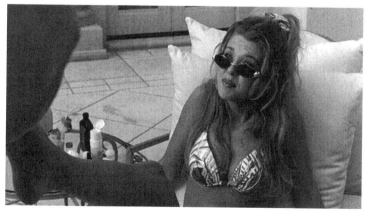

Bums: Were you aware that *The Big Lebowski* had such a big following? Why do you think people are so devoted to the film?

TR: It's a total cult movie; people love it. Someone told me there is even a *Big Lebowski* festival, where people dress up as the characters of the movie.

Bums: Thanks, Tara, we're just gonna go find a cash machine.

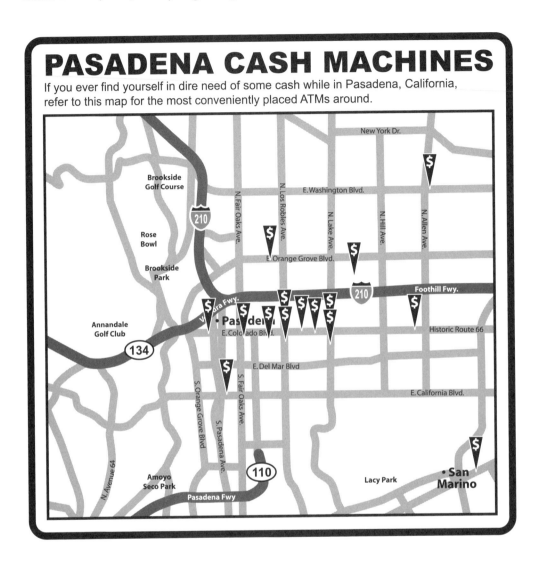

ASIA CARRERA

Name: Asia Carrera

Character: Sherry in *Logjammin'*

Born: New York, August 6, 1973

Select Filmography: *Bangkok Boobarella*, *Best of Male Domination 23*, *Hotel No Tell*, *Improper Conduct*, *New Positions*, *Butt Watch 5*, *Putting It All Behind 2*, *Seymore Butts in Buttland*

Trivia: Asia has an IQ of 156 and is a member of Mensa.

A version of this interview with Asia Carrera appeared at MrSkin.com. Reprinted by permission.

Q: I found nowhere on your site where you talked about your experience working on *The Big Lebowski*. How did you land that gig?

Asia Carrera: I got a call from a talent agent that they were looking to cast a porn star for a Coen brothers movie. They asked me to come in and take some Polaroid shots. So I showed up, posed in some lingerie, and that was it—no reading lines or anything.

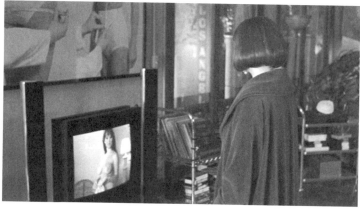

Q: Then what happened?

AC: After I took the pics, the agent said to me, "You are very beautiful—too beautiful for this part, probably. The Coen brothers prefer more quirky, real looks in their characters." I was disappointed, but if I was going to be rejected for being too beautiful, that wasn't a bad way to go, right?

Q: Yeah. Beats the alternative.

AC: So the very next day I got a phone call from the agent saying that the Coen brothers came down and pointed out my shots. They said [to the agent]: "That's the one we want!" So I got the part!

Q: So when did you start production?

AC: The day I shot my scene with them was actually the first day of the whole movie. Everyone was nervous, and all the bigwigs and all the moneymen were on the set. I didn't know that, though, so it didn't intimidate me at all. I just did my thing. Everyone thought I was cute.

Q: And that's it?

AC: Just wait a minute! So the brothers stopped shooting and wrote some dialogue for me. That way I could get my SAG card out of the gig, because originally my part didn't have any dialogue. When they watched the dailies later, they were impressed that I could deliver my lines exactly the same with my top on, and with it off.

Q: Funny, isn't that why they hired you?

AC: Totally. But then came the kicker: I got a request from the agent to autograph about a dozen eight-by-tens for all the bigwigs who'd been on set that day—including the brothers. Everyone was too shy and intimidated to ask me to my face!

JESSE FLANAGAN

Name: Jesse Flanagan
Character: Little Larry Sellers
Born: Santa Monica, California, April 14, 1982
Select Filmography: *Art School Confidential*, *The Modern Adventures of Tom Sawyer*
Trivia: Jesse has appeared in many television commercials, including one where he is prevented from vandalizing a bicycle by McGruff the Crime Dog.

Bums: How did you get the part?

Jesse Flanagan: I got the part from one of the most interesting auditions that I can remember. All they asked me to do was stay seated while they cursed at me and did all types of ranting and raving. I'm guessing they wanted to see who could stonewall the best and not crack under pressure, and, well, as you can tell from the movie, I am pretty darn good at it.

Bums: What did they tell you about your character and part?

JF: Basically they told me I was a teenager who lashed out doing things that weren't necessarily bad but weren't good either. They told me I didn't have much of an at-home role model, and wasn't getting the best parenting, and to take what I could from that.

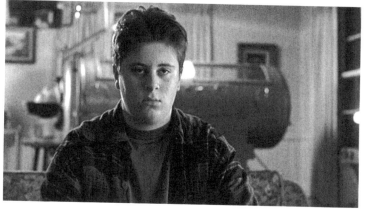

Bums: Was John Goodman scary when he was yelling at you?

JF: John Goodman was a riot to work with. He brought everything he could to his character and then some. Let's put it like this: The audition was hard, but when John Goodman came into the room on the first take, it was almost impossible not to crack up.

I've gotten many requests to stonewall.

Bums: Do people recognize you on the street?

JF: People seem to recognize me everywhere I go from that role. I've gotten many requests to stonewall. It's just great to see everyone so in love with the movie.

One of my favorite times that I can recall was when I was with a few friends, and a guy that I had never met came out of a store. He looked at me and said, "Where's the money, you little brat?" My friends were actually shocked because they didn't recall what the guy was talking about. But it happens a lot to me, so I knew exactly what he was talking about. It was a great moment.

Bums: If you had to guess, how many times has someone asked, "Is this your homework, Larry?"

JF: Realistically I couldn't put an exact number, but over the years I would have to say it's a four-, maybe even five-digit number.

Bums: Is this your homework, Larry?

JF: Yes. Yes, it is my homework.

JIM HOOSIER

Name: Jim Hoosier

Character: Liam O'Brien (The Jesus's bowling buddy)

Born: Ventura, California, December 31, 1952

Complete Filmography: *The Big Lebowski*

Trivia: Jim is quite the bowler—his high game is 299.

Bums: How did you get involved with *The Big Lebowski?*

Jim Hoosier: I answered a flyer at a local bowling center. They were looking for someone in their forties who looked Irish. I went down and answered a couple questions from the receptionist, and she took my picture and told me if the directors were interested they would contact me.

A couple days later I got a call. When I arrived for this meeting, the Coen brothers were there. They asked me how I had heard about the part. I told them my story. They asked if I would change my appearance, and I told them anything they wanted I would do. Then Joel looked at me and said, "See, Jim, it's not that hard to get into the movies, is it?" They called me two weeks later and offered me the part.

Bums: Was it hard for you to keep a straight face when John Turturro showed up on the set in his Jesus jumpsuit?

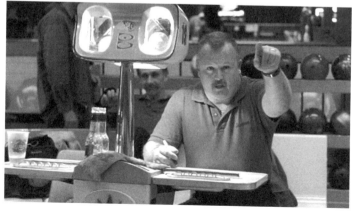

JH: Hey, I was wearing a shirt and pants that were two sizes too small! How much laughing could I do? I really was out of my element there. I was not an actor and had no idea how to act.

When John came onto the set he was introduced to John Goodman, Jeff Bridges, and Steve Buscemi, and I just walked right along with him and shook hands also.

Bums: What was your initial reaction to the fans at Lebowski Fest?

JH: The first Fest that I attended was in Vegas. I had a couple of buddies with me. The first night we were walking through the casino, and I could see people looking at me and pointing. My buddies noticed it also, but didn't say anything.

When we got upstairs someone said, "That's Liam!" and we looked at each other and cracked up. I could not believe that these people knew who I was! Inside the meeting room, people started calling my name and asking for autographs and taking pictures. It was all so totally humbling.

My next fest was in L.A., and this time I had my family with me. The fans started calling my name as we were entering the Knitting Factory, and my wife fell out. I had told her about Vegas, but she didn't believe me. By the time Saturday night at the bowling alley was over, she had even had her picture taken with fans who wanted Liam's wife. It was all too much to believe. I am in complete awe of this whole ride.

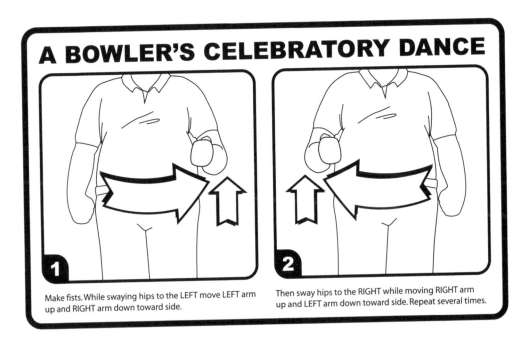

A BOWLER'S CELEBRATORY DANCE

1 Make fists. While swaying hips to the LEFT move LEFT arm up and RIGHT arm down toward side.

2 Then sway hips to the RIGHT while moving RIGHT arm up and LEFT arm down toward side. Repeat several times.

JERRY HALEVA

Name: Jerry Haleva
Character: Saddam Hussein
Born: Portland, Oregon, May 26, 1946
Select Filmography: *Live from Baghdad, Mafia, Hot Shots!, Hot Shots! Part Deux*
Trivia: Jerry has six acting credits; all of them are as Saddam Hussein.

Bums: How did you get involved with *The Big Lebowski?*

Jerry Haleva: I received a call from Joel Coen—at first I didn't believe it was him!—who informed me that they were making a movie with Jeff Bridges and there was a small part for Saddam Hussein. Jeff had told him to "get the guy who acted with my dad in *Hot Shots!*" Being a huge fan of the Coen brothers, I was thrilled to be asked.

Bums: How many times have you played Saddam on the screen?

JH: I have appeared or costarred in six feature films. While clearly my costarring role in *Hot Shots! Part Deux* was the biggest part. I think I've gained as much attention from my fifteen seconds in *The Big Lebowski.*

Bums: How did you get started as a Saddam lookalike?

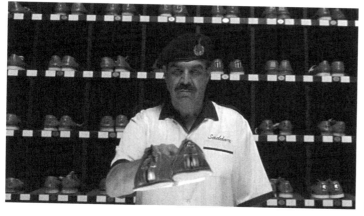

JH: In 1989, the chief sergeant at arms for the California State Senate, where I worked, saw a photo of Saddam in the *L.A. Times.* He distributed a copy of the photo to the members of the state senate with the caption, "Now we know what Haleva does on his weekends!" I was subsequently contacted by a lookalike agent, and the rest is history.

Bums: What else do you do for a living?

JH: After more than twenty years as a professional staff member to the California legislature, in 1990 I opened my own lobbying and consulting business, Sergeant Major Associates. My company currently represents more than a dozen clients on regulatory and legislative matters both in Sacramento and Washington, D.C.

Bums: What do the politicians say about your likeness to Saddam? What about Cheney?

JH: My resemblance has been a huge hook that allows me to be remembered by politicians who meet hundreds of people each week. Cheney, like most politicians I have met on both sides of the aisle, has a great sense of humor and appreciates the irony of a pro-Israel Jewish activist getting to play an evil Arab dictator.

Bums: How do you think your lookalike career will be affected now that Saddam's verdict has been carried out?

JH: I won't be hanging around for very long.

ROBIN JONES

Name: Robin Jones
Character: Ralphs Checkout Girl
Born: Boston, February 22
Select Filmography: *One Flight Stand, Cupids, Howards End*
Trivia: Robin practices Krav Maga, a style of hand-to-hand combat developed by the Israeli army.

Bums: How did you get involved in the movie?

Robin Jones: I saw an ad in *Backstage West*. They kept running this ad saying they were looking for someone to do this role. Not that the Coen brothers don't care about hygiene, but I knew the style of the Coen brothers, so I sent in pictures that were very unflattering.

Bums: So it specified "Coen brothers movie"?

RJ: Exactly. It was almost too good to be true, but I thought, Well, sure. I did my little A-student thing and followed the directions and mailed it, and finally I just had to let it go because I didn't hear anything. And I thought, Yeah, it was too good to be true. It was probably a hoax.

And then I got a call, and they said, "We'd like you to come in and audition. But

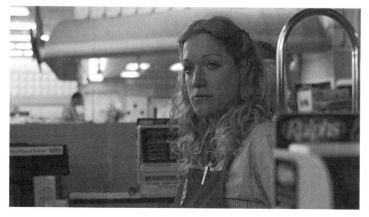

we're telling people that the role is not glamorous, so don't wear makeup and don't do your hair and don't wear your best outfit."

So I didn't wash my hair. I don't think I bathed. And I just put on the swampiest thing

I had and didn't brush my hair. And frankly, I think I was the only person who followed the directions. Because everybody there showed up looking *gorgeous*. And I was like, "Yeah!"

So when they called, they said the shoot was going to go from nine p.m. to three a.m. at a Ralphs in Pasadena. When I showed up, everything was parked in the parking lot, and there were the Coen brothers sitting there.

So it was really small—it was just me and Jeff Bridges sitting there getting makeup done. It was *incredible*. He said that next time he won't gain weight for a role, he'll just wear padding, because he had gotten himself this big belly for the role and he said it was just impossible to get rid of. And I was

> **One is saying, "Now, Robin, I want you to look there, and I want you to look over there. Now chew your gum."**

like, "*Blech,* who is this disgusting—oh, it's Jeff Bridges!" And Holly Hunter was there. She was just hanging out with them at this odd hour of the night.

Bums: That's so funny. You, Jeff Bridges, Holly Hunter, and Joel and Ethan Coen?

RJ: Yeah, I mean really, that was it. And they were just totally casual. They talked me through the whole thing without sound. They just did filming. So instead of letting me go deeply into character [*jokingly*] and act, they just *talked* the whole time. While I'm standing there and while Jeff is coming toward me, Ethan and Joel are just talking constantly.

One is saying, "Now, Robin, I want you to look there, and I want you to look over there. Now chew your gum. Okay, now chew your gum." So it looks like I'm just silent and staring, but really I've got these two guys talking at me the whole time.

And then it was time for my close-up, which is the only thing that made it in the film anyway, and Jeff Bridges *left*! So I had to stare at space! As they were filming, I was thinking, "I'm really not looking at him. He's not there. He's having a frappé and a back rub!"

But they kept talking. Every time they ever gave me a direction, Joel or Ethan, they would laugh. They would say, "Have her do this—*ha ha ha ha!*" They love their own humor so much, they really didn't need anyone else to be there. They already thought that what they were doing was totally hilarious, and it was like two guys having fun: "Now go stand over there. *Ha ha ha ha!*" [*mockingly*] They were very sure that they were hilarious guys. And they are. And neither of them looked like they had showered in weeks.

They were both wearing hooded sweatshirts, and Joel had really long hair in a ponytail. It was all very, very *casual*.

Bums: So that's amazing that people recognize you almost on a daily basis.

RJ: It's so funny. Everybody says, "You've gotta tell me which Ralphs that was!" And I get stopped all the time about that. It's *amazing* how many people have a religion around the movie. I mean, a *religion*. And then how many people would even notice a split second of some checker girl.

Like just the other day, my sister and I—growing up we never dressed like twins, but now as adults we enjoy doing it. And we walked into an office building, and the guy at the front desk said, "Oh, my God! Which one of you is Robin?"

And so I said, "Well, I'm Robin."

And he didn't explain himself. He just stuck out his hand and started shaking my hand. And I'm thinking, Huh?

And he said, "I'm a big fan of the film."

And we're identical twins, dressed up in little red minidresses with our hair all poofy and really high heels and just totally Barbie-dolled up. *Identical twins*. So that's a whole other persona that usually is a heavy *pow*! when we walk in the door—it's like a visual shock.

So for him to *ignore* that, ignore the fact that we were dressed up like Barbie-hooker identical twins—that didn't impress him at all. He couldn't care less. He wasn't attracted to us. He didn't think it was interesting that we were twins. He just *immediately* realized that one of them was the checker girl in *The Big Lebowski*! That was *bizarre*. And he knew the checker girl's *real name*? That was the weirdest thing. He didn't even look at my sister. He didn't introduce himself to my sister. He didn't shake her hand. He didn't care.

STEVE BUSCEMI

Name: Steve Buscemi

Character: Donny

Born: Brooklyn, December 13, 1957

Select Filmography: *Interview, Big Fish, Ghost World, Trees Lounge, Fargo, The Hudsucker Proxy, Reservoir Dogs, Barton Fink, Miller's Crossing, Mystery Train*

Trivia: Steve was a New York City fireman in the 1980s.

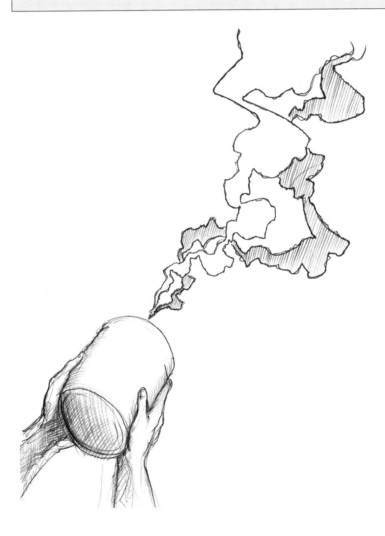

CHAPTER THREE

WAY OUT WEST.
ORIGINS AND
INSPIRATIONS

As anyone who has ever seen a Coen brothers movie can tell you, it's sometimes possible to take things too far. Like Walter when he pulls the Big Lebowski from his wheelchair, you can get in trouble. But it can also be funny. We'd heard that many of the characters in *The Big Lebowski* were inspired by actual people and that some of the key sequences were inspired by actual events. Being rabid fans, we were curious. We were writing a fan book, after all. We wanted to know. But how far was too far? Would trying to pin the movie down to a set of facts and dates lessen its charm?

Luckily, that wasn't a problem. We were, in fact, able to track down a number of the people who inspired characters in the movie, following a trail that eventually led all the way to the *real* "Little Larry" Sellers. (Who, as it turned out, had absolutely no idea he held that honor until he listened to a message we left him on his mother's answering machine.) But as far as facts go, forget about it. What we eventually learned was that the word *inspirations* is the one that fits best. "Little Larry" is not actually a fucking dunce. "The Dude" was never a roadie for Metallica.

In recording the interviews you'll find below, we found we had to forget about trying

Look!
A Little Larry
flip book!

to connect the dots. What we were left with were the stories and the extremely interesting, funny people who were telling them. And at that point it was easy to see why *The Big Lebowski* is one of the great comedies of modern times: because it was, from the beginning, all about laughter. It started with stories that had the Coen brothers laughing so hard they were falling out of their chairs. By the time we'd finished with these interviews, we'd fallen out of our chairs a few times, too.

A (Not Quite) Interview with the Coen Brothers

Bums: Can we interview you guys about *The Big Lebowski* for a fan book we're writing?

Coen brothers (via their friend Peter Exline): We let you borrow the marmot.* Don't push it.

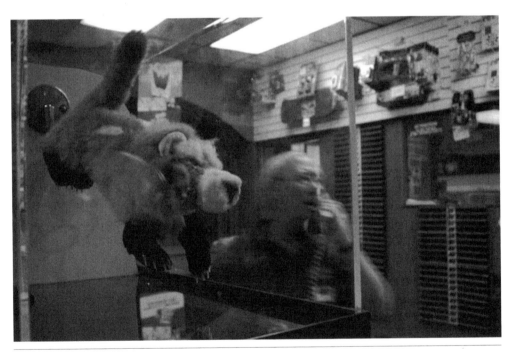

---

* In 2003, the Coen brothers graciously allowed us to borrow the prop marmot that they used in the bathtub scene to display at the Third Annual Lebowski Fest in Louisville, Kentucky, in exchange for two Achiever T-shirts and a poster. The fake marmot was mounted inside a glass case with an engraved plaque that read MARMOT ON A STICK, and a PVC tube extending from its tiny rodentlike rear with a drill attachment on the end. Apparently the drill attachment was used to "spin" the fake animal in the bathtub water.

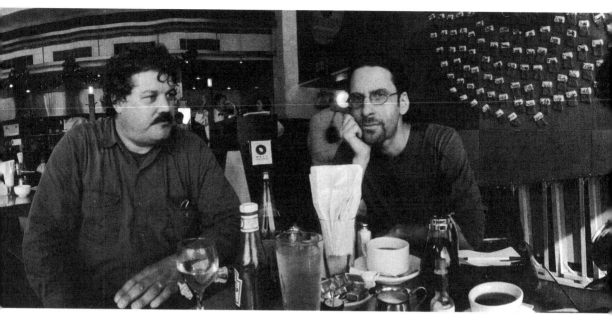

JEFF "THE DUDE" DOWD: He's the Dude. So That's What You Call Him.

Jeff Dowd is the man around whom the Coen brothers loosely modeled the character of the Dude. Dowd was a political activist in the sixties and a member of the Seattle Seven (him and six other guys). Jeff Bridges met with Dowd as filming began and was able to mimic Dowd's body language and speaking mannerisms perfectly.

Jeff Dowd is not a lazy man. He has been working in film production for nearly thirty years and helped land distribution deals for a number of high-profile independent films including the Coens' first film, *Blood Simple*. He has also appeared at many Lebowski Fests to enjoy some White Russians and roll a few with fellow Achievers.

As a result of *The Big Lebowski*'s popularity, Dowd has found himself greeted by fans as an icon in his own right. He tells stories of being recognized by *Lebowski* fans around the world, from army colonels to Wall Street bankers to musicians and professional athletes of every stripe. And the Dude *does* know how to tell a story. In fact, he's in the process of finishing a manuscript of his own called *The Dude Abides: Classic Tales and Rebel Rants*.

JD: Joel and Ethan and I met because it was the first year of Sundance. There happened to be a guy there who was giving money into some of Redford's environmental causes, but he'd also put some money into the limited partnership of *Blood Simple*. And he asked Redford, "What should I do about this movie?" And Redford said he should talk to me, and told me a little bit about the movie.

Several months later, I was in New York City and I happened to be at the Fox office wearing a jacket and tie, because that's what you do in New York. And Joel and Ethan show up. It's September. They're all grungy-looking and everything, and they're obviously there because one of the investors said, "Maybe you ought to check this out." They were pretty uninterested. They weren't totally enthusiastic about pitching me this. *Blood Simple* is a pretty tough movie to describe, right?

And so we met for a while, and they left, and I could tell that it didn't go real well. And who knows when some indie guys pitch you something, right? They weren't trying real hard. I looked like the suit from Fox to them.

> And whenever they would talk to me, they would get on the phone and I'd hear this stereo version of, "Dude? Duder? Duderino?"

So by chance later that night, I'm walking in Greenwich Village and I run into them again. And now I've got my leather jacket on, and we talk on the street for a few minutes, and then by even more fate, about one in the morning I was at an IFC party at a loft in the Village, and there they were again. So we had a couple of drinks. At that point we knew there was some destiny working.

So in due course they showed me the movie. In the first few minutes I went, "Wow! These guys are real filmmakers." You could tell right away. They had a real kind of unique voice and style. And so they asked me to represent the film, which I did. And we spent the next quite a few months, almost a year, getting turned down by every distributor three times. Every single one. They all looked at it and shrugged their shoulders and went, "No."

We spent a lot of time. I remembered the other day that New Line and New World both turned us down on the same day. And we said, let's just go get a bottle of Jack Daniel's and we'll rent *Bring Me the Head of Alfredo Garcia*.

One of the discoveries I made at that point is that you couldn't really show a black comedy to people without an audience. We finally arranged to show it at the Toronto Film Festival, where probably about eight hundred people were. And then an amazing thing happened: People started laughing. And then we had a minor bidding war, and we ended up selling the film.

Bums: Do you remember at what point they found out that you called yourself the Dude?

JD: The story on the Dude is I started to be referred to as the Dude in sixth grade when I was living in Berkeley, California, and two guys on a baseball team named Abe and Danny started calling me the Dude. And then when my father moved us back East, kids there started calling me the Dude, too, based on my size and stuff like that.

Unlike in the movie, where Bridges tells people to refer to him as the Dude, I never did that. But that name then started to pick up and people started to use it. And then, years later during the war movement, we would go to these conventions and all the guys from Cornell would refer to me as the Dude. And so people started to use that name.

So people from around the country in the SDS [Students for a Democratic Society] started calling me the Dude and hearing that name. Our chapter was kind of like the coolest chapter: best organized, and we partied the best. So that name got attached to Jeff Dowd.

So Joel and Ethan are so well read that they read that in some article or some book. And one day, they called me on the phone—they used to like to get on the phone together—and Ethan said, "Dude? Duder? Duderino?" And whenever they would talk to me, they would get on the phone and I'd hear this stereo version of, "Dude? Duder? Duderino?" All the stuff that's in the movie. They just liked riffing on the name a lot.

Bums: What parts of the movie were actually based on your life?

JD: I was never a roadie for Metallica! Although, ironically, I ended up working with them on their movie.

Basically, I think what Joel and Ethan were doing is, they wanted to create—as is the

Me and six other guys

The Seattle Seven, also known as the Seattle Liberation Front, was started in 1970 by University of Washington professor Micheal Lerner as a result of the breakup of Students for a Democratic Society. Members included Micheal Abeles, Joe Kelly, Micheal Justesen, Susan Stern, Roger Lippman, Jeff Dowd, and Chip Marshall.

case in many great movies—these opposites. And there is almost always one guy who gets the other guy in trouble.

So, you know, Butch is always getting Sundance in trouble. Tony Curtis is getting Jack Lemmon in trouble in *Some Like It Hot*. Mel Gibson is getting Danny Glover in trouble in *Lethal Weapon*. And so Walter is the guy who is always pushing and getting the Dude in trouble.

And they froze two guys in time. They froze what we might've been like, and we were a little bit like that to a large extent in the seventies for a year or two, after the political activism died down and before we went back to work. We were hanging pretty heavy in Seattle. And we were, indeed, drinking White Russians for a while, somewhere in between tequila sunrises and dirty mothers and Harvey Wallbangers.

> **When my kids saw the poster of the movie, they said, "Daddy, where'd they get your clothes?"**

Bums: Do you remember how the Coens picked up that little detail about the White Russians?

JD: That I don't know. But what you should know, though, is how all this stuff came up. Writers write what's funny. Or they write where there's conflict. And White Russian is a funny name for a drink. You can riff on it.

They like stuff they can take from and do something with. Very early on, I asked them, "How do you guys write?" And Joel said, "Well, I'll write a scene and I'll make it as difficult as I possibly can for the character." And Ethan said, "And I'll make it worse." And then Joel said, "And then I'll make it worse again."

Making the situation worse is what all great drama and all great comedy is going to come out of. So if you look at *The Big Lebowski*, or you look at *Fargo*, or you look at *Raising Arizona*, you'll see how things progress: Things get worse and worse and worse.

As for the bowling thing, I can give you my take on why I think that happened. When we opened *Blood Simple* in L.A., I was in charge of the L.A. party because I lived there and I had an idea that I thought was interesting: to throw a party at a bowling alley. And this is before bowling alleys became trendy. I thought it might be an interesting location.

So I found a little bowling alley in Santa Monica, and it turned out that the upstairs bar, this big room that had been sealed for years, had actually been the secret hideaway for the Rat Pack. Sammy Davis Jr. and Sinatra and Dean Martin would stay there on their way to Peter Lawford's place about a mile away in Santa Monica. And this was like their own little place. Nobody knew that.

And that night at the party we had bands and music—almost like Lebowski Fest—and it was really rockin'. And I rolled a few, of both kinds, and everybody was having a great time. And I think it was pretty much there that Joel and Ethan observed me bowling and saw this kind of wild time and camaraderie that takes place, and they got the idea for the Dude bowling.

Bums: Just a little bit more about the character of the Dude. What parts of the character that Jeff Bridges portrayed did he get from you?

JD: He got all the physicality. But it's not just Jeff. It's also Joel and Ethan. When my kids saw the poster of the movie, they said, "Daddy, where'd they get your clothes?" Those weren't my clothes, but the costume designer got it, you know?

I mean, that's what good directors do: They work with pretty much the same team on every movie, right? And so she got that, and so did Bridges. *All* the physicality. The slouching, the belly, the clothes. In the original script it describes the Dude as a man "in whom casualness runs deep."

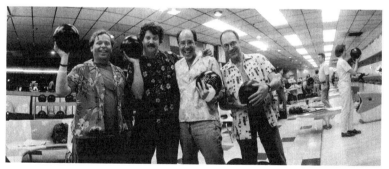

The car, by the way: In the original script it actually called for the car I used to have, which was a Chrysler LeBaron convertible. When it came time to shoot the movie, they couldn't get Goodman into a Chrysler LeBaron. I mean, you could *shoehorn* the guy in there, but it wasn't big enough so that he could turn and look at the Dude. So they needed a big car like a Torino, because the LeBaron wouldn't fit for Goodman.

The phrase "Dude here" comes from one time I was at the Venice Film Festival with *Blood Simple* and they weren't there, but they knew to call the hospitality suite to look for me. And the phone kept ringing, and I picked up the phone and said, "Dude here." And they got that line right there.

Bums: So let's talk a little bit about the fans and the cult following that has grown up around this film. Do you have any theories on what it is about the movie that has spawned this reaction in different people?

JD: To some degree. I know because I talk to an awful lot of people, and some in different ways than you guys. You guys see them mainly in the context of Lebowski Fest, but I see them everywhere. Often in different countries, even. I see a lot of them at Lebowski festivals, but also a lot of people who haven't been to Lebowski Fest. They did a *Lebowski* showing at Berkeley last week.

So there are a few things. Obviously you're taking a situation where the film didn't do that well in theaters for various reasons but took off as a DVD. And then it ended up having this following. The figure I heard is that it has sold something like twenty million DVDs.

Anyhow. It's a lot of things. People like to repeat the lines of *The Big Lebowski*. Because they're such memorable and classic lines. And of course you can use them, as we've seen, in all kinds of other contexts. And people do that all the time. I've even heard that there's a Wall Street firm that when they're interviewing people, they throw out a few of the lines in the interview and see if people pick up on them, and they don't hire them if they don't.

Then, this is a movie you can see with your friends. Or your family. It is really enjoyable to see with other people. And it doesn't matter: You can be drunk, stoned, baked, it doesn't matter. It's a movie you know you're going to feel *better* while watching the movie or after the movie than you felt at the beginning.

I talked to a family that watches it on Thanksgiving. After dinner, the whole twenty-five of them get together and watch *The Big Lebowski*. And these aren't a bunch of hippie types, but they watch it because they just know it's going to make them feel better. And they've been doing it for five or six years now. And that's the tradition, instead of watching the Detroit Lions football game. Which is *not* going to make them feel better, particularly if you're a Detroit Lions fan.

Or then there is the story of the 9/11 fireman. He's a volunteer fireman who was at 9/11. He'd seen people die before and he'd saved people's lives before, but he'd never seen people taking their own lives as they did when they were jumping out of the buildings. And he lost a lot of friends who were firemen that day. He was absolutely psychologically devastated. His life went to pieces. He was a horrible husband, he was yelling at his kids, and he went to doctors and shrinks and took all kinds of pills.

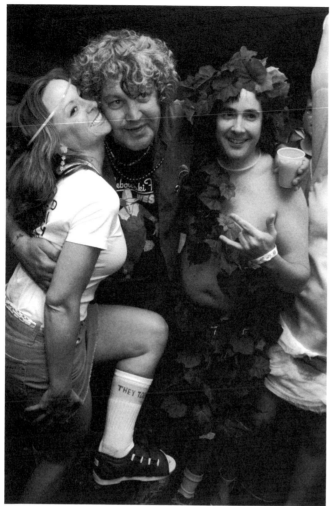

And then one day, about six or seven months later after 9/11, he's sitting there in his living room—he wasn't working at the time—and he looked on his shelf and he spotted the DVD of *The Big Lebowski*. And he put it in the DVD player and started watching it. And he said, "For the first time in six months, I smiled and I started laughing." And he kept laughing. And he watched it again and again. So *The Big Lebowski* was the thing, the drug, if you will, that brought him out of his posttraumatic stress syndrome.

The other phenomenon is, I think, the DVD revolution, so to speak. If you're traveling and you have five or ten DVDs, *The Big Lebowski* is often one of them. Which means *everybody* on every sports team has seen that movie. You cannot find athletes, or guys who travel, who haven't. Guys in the army, rock 'n' roll bands, all of them, they all watch the film again and again.

It's like a great record album. Some record albums have two or three hits on them. And some have twelve or thirteen. And in the sequence of *The Big Lebowski*, there are like ten or twelve great classic sequences. The Jesus sequence, Larry Sellers—there are so many of them.

So you've got all these things working at once: watching it together, repeated viewings, and then it's just one of the few DVDs. And you put that all together. And it's also a common discovery. People bond on their values. And when friends discover that they both like *The Big Lebowski*, kind of like you guys did, it becomes a bond. They can watch it together, or talk about it. It's just like when you find a baseball team that you both like, or a band that you both like. You find this movie that you both like.

But I'm not so sure that you have people talking at length about how they both like Brad Pitt. Even though he's a very good actor. Or George Clooney. You know, George Clooney is a great actor, he's a great director, he's a great producer, but I don't think you've had too many conversations that last too long, more than a few sentences, between anybody—between women who might find him cute or anybody—those kinds of conversations don't usually last more than a minute. A *Big Lebowski* conversation can last an hour.

Bums: So what's it like to be the Dude?

JD: It's this great gift, this icon status that Joel and Ethan have laid on me. It allows me a platform to do political and cultural and spiritual discussions. And so I think I've turned it into a really good thing. And I try not to abuse it too much.

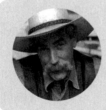

The Stranger Says . . .

"Dude here." The Dude is in every scene except for the one where the nihilists have breakfast.

PETER EXLINE: His Rug Really Tied the Room Together. His Car Was Also Stolen. (Separate Incidents.)

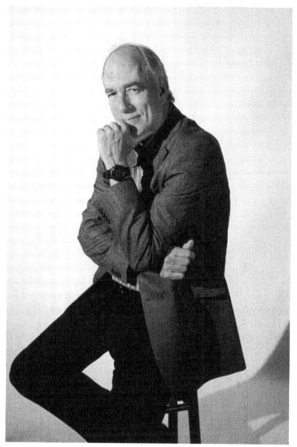

We first learned of Peter Exline via an e-mail from one of his students. She told us that he was one of the inspirations for the story line of *The Big Lebowski* as well as one of the inspirations for Walter. Exline, she told us, is a film professor at USC, and she went on to relate how once while pacing back and forth during a lecture, he bumped into a chair. After bumping into it several times, he finally got fed up and threw it across the room, shouting, *"First Vietnam, now this chair!"*

Exline met the Coen brothers at a Super Bowl party and later, while playing host to them at a small get-together in his backyard, told them a story about how his car was stolen and then recovered—with the addition of an eighth grader's homework stuffed between the seats. While telling the Coens this story, he would often pause and point out how the new rug he had recently acquired "really tied the room together." The Coens call him the "Philosopher King of Hollywood." This is the story of his rug, his stolen car, and his visit to an eighth-grade delinquent. It made us laugh to beat the band.

Peter Exline: Barry Sonnenfeld and I were buddies at NYU, and I was working for a producer in Beverly Hills, Mace Neufeld. Barry introduced me to Joel and Ethan. They were trying to raise money for this screenplay they'd written called *Blood Simple*. And later that year, I was back in New York for a birthday party, and it was Super Bowl Sunday, and Barry had me over—along with Joel and Ethan. I think that's when my humor kind of charmed them.

> **Every now and then I'd stop and I'd say, "Doesn't this rug tie the room together?" And everybody laughed.**

I think I kind of won them over because of the way I teased Barry. I was the suit from Beverly Hills when they first met me, and they were trying to figure out how to play this. And then when they saw that I was actually pretty funny and kind of abusive toward Barry, they kind of said, well, this guy's gotta be okay.

So I had them over for dinner and a neighbor had moved out, and I'd gone over and scoped out their place and saw this old faux-Persian rug on their floor. Now, any New Yorker worth his salt knows that if somebody has left behind furniture, that means, "I don't want it. You can have it." I knew people in New York who had decorated entire apartments without ever buying any furniture. They decorated their entire apartments with what they saw on the street and what the neighbors had left behind. So I had rolled this faux-Persian rug up and laid it down in my living room, and I was joking to them about how it tied the room together. And Joel and Ethan were there and some other friends were there with their girlfriends and wives, and I was barbecuing some chicken and telling this story about my car being stolen.

You know how you milk a joke? All night long, I kept talking about Lew [Abernathy, a friend of Exline's who was also an inspiration for Walter, see interview page 106] and my car, and I'd stop and I'd say, "Doesn't this rug really tie the room together?" Every time I said it I got a laugh. Joel and Ethan just seem to think I'm so funny.

But my car had been stolen, and Lew and I were buddies. Although we didn't call him Lew. We called him Big Lew.

Bums: He was a private investigator, is that right?

PE: He had done everything. He was a Vietnam vet. He had fought in Angola. He said he almost got killed in Angola by a fuckin' Russian hand grenade. Then he worked in a photo shop, developing, and these private investigators would bring in this really bad footage, and he said, "You know, I could do this." So he became a private investigator trying to catch husbands cheating on their wives and wives cheating on their husbands.

And then he went to USC, the Peter Stark program, which is a really elite graduate school. Especially for producers, and kids are kind of guaranteed to get a job when they graduate. And then Lew crewed and wrote, and he sold a script. John Cunningham directed it—*Deep Star Six*.

He's this big Vietnam vet, and we'd have breakfast on Santa Monica Boulevard in West L.A. at a place called the Cafe 50's that had a 1950s motif. It's still up there. So my car gets stolen, and Mr. former private eye Lew Abernathy says, "No, you'll never see your car again." Because he knew—he knew because he's a private investigator. "You know, it's some guy, he ran out of gas, he jumped into your car, you live near the freeway, he jumped into your car, he's headed to San Francisco or Bakersfield or God knows where, and he's just gonna dump it and grab another one. You're never going to see your car again."

So ten days later I got a letter from the L.A. police department. My car had been impounded. I had about a half a dozen parking tickets. It was in an impound yard really close by. So I called Lew, and we go down to the car. And it's pretty beat-up—the front left tire is gone, and they got that little fake spare tire out of the trunk on there, and it looks like a little rubber toy tire. And the backseat is filled with junk. There was a basketball and a Hard Rock Las Vegas T-shirt, and there are all these fast-food wrappers.

So I reach into the trunk and there is a cassette in there, a homemade soul tape. So I'm looking at it, and I happen to know of this cult in Brentwood. There was a guy who was a former schoolteacher who had decided that he's the 375th reincarnation of Jesus Christ. So he's got this cult, and it was a tape of the soul, you know. It wasn't Aretha Franklin. It wasn't Motown.

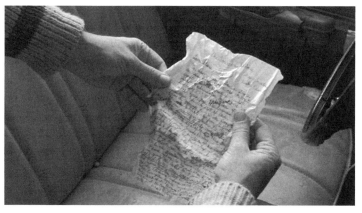

So Lew makes this big pronouncement. He's determined that there are three guys who stole my car. He said there are three of them and the guy in the backseat is really big. Like, the only guy who ate any food was the guy in the backseat. And the other two guys just drove him around to Burger King.

So I'm telling this story and I'm barbecuing, and my buddies are there, and Joel and Ethan are there, and, like I said—every now and then I'd stop and I'd say, "Doesn't this rug tie the room together?" And everybody laughed.

So then Lew on his own reaches under the passenger seat of the car. He pulls out this eighth grader's homework.

Bums: Oh, my God.

PE: And it's Jaik Freeman. And naturally Lew says, "Well, you'll never find *this* kid." And you may have noticed that Lew has been wrong about everything. "You'll never see your car again." "There're three of them." And that's the point of my story. That's why I'm telling it to Joel and Ethan.

Now, I'm sure that when Lew told you about the car, he had a very different take on it.

Bums: Yes. He was right. He thought that he had gotten straight to the correct version of events.

PE: Of course. That's the other thing about Lew: He's like George Bush—he's always right. If there had been mistakes in the past, Lew didn't make 'em. So, now, I know one fourteen-year-old kid in all of L.A. And he hangs out down at the convenience store where I get beer and cigarettes and soda and cups of coffee. So I go down to West Side Junior convenience store that night and there's Nick, the only fourteen-year-old kid I know in all of L.A. So I say, "Nick, hey, how you doing? Do you hang out with Jaik Freeman?" And he backs up a step, looks at me, and says, "Nooooo . . ."

And as I'm leaving I say, "So, where do you go to school?" And he names the school, and it's about six blocks from my apartment. So I go home and I get out the phone book and I start calling all the Freemans: "Hi, I'm looking for the parents of Jaik Freeman that goes to such-and-such junior high."

And the eleventh phone call this woman says, "Yeah?"

And I say, "Mrs. Freeman, hi, I'm Peter Exline, I live at Ohio and Greenfield. My car was recently stolen, and it has been recovered, and I have found your son's homework in my car."

And she says, "Oh, my God."

And so now I'm talking to Mrs. Freeman and I'm trying to save her son from a life of

"My car was recently stolen, and it has been recovered, and I have found your son's homework in my car."

crime. And probably trying to get five hundred dollars out of her. Because I figured my car is totaled or close to it, and my deductible is five hundred dollars. So I make a date to go over there Friday night. And I call Lew, and Lew comes and picks me up, and we drive over there. And it's a real nice neighborhood. It's Westwood. And we're driving down the street and I'm looking at a piece of paper, the directions, and I say, "Okay, it's that house," and Lew drives by it. I say, "Lew, what are you doing? The house is back there."

And he says, "I want to make sure there's not a setup."

"So this housewife has got a team of ninjas in the trees?"

So he performs an illegal U-turn, and we go up and knock on the door. And it's this really nice two-story Spanish house, and Mrs. Freeman comes to the door. Mrs. Freeman is English, she's in her fifties, very Tiffany, very well appointed—she's got a nice oxford-cloth dress shirt and a teal-green sweater, and beautiful silver-blond hair and a pageboy haircut. She's not all that happy to see Big Lew.

So Mrs. Freeman lets us into the house, and little Jaik waddles down, little kid from the second floor, not too happy to see us, and I notice the house is a little bit cramped, a little bit dusty. Nothing excessive. We go from this little foyer into the living room, and my eyes practically pop out of my head because across the living room where most people have a fireplace is a hospital bed and a guy in the hospital bed—seventy-five, eighty years old—chain-smoking unfiltered Camel cigarettes, reading underneath a rack of track lighting.

So we start talking, I'm telling my story. And I didn't even notice it, but Lew has a briefcase. Now he flips open this briefcase and he brings up a Whopper wrapper in a baggie. He's holding this up like he's Perry Mason in front of a jury. And then he slides that back into his briefcase and I'm talking, and he pulls out another baggie, and this one is Jaik's homework. And he gets up and he walks over to Jaik and stands right in front of him. He says, "We know you did it, Jaik. We know you took the car." And he shows him this homework.

When I told this at the dinner party, Joel and Ethan almost gagged. They were laughing so hard that this guy has got Whopper wrappers and homework in baggies. This part particularly inflamed their laughing motors.

So, you know, I finish my presentation and Mrs. Freeman says, very nicely, very politely, "Well, my son loaned his math book to another kid and the kid never returned it. He's never been in your car. He didn't steal your car. He does have an idea who might have stolen your car, and if the police call and ask, we'll be glad to tell them."

So I'm thinking, okay, she's talked to a lawyer and she's well aware of her rights and her position. She doesn't have to give us any information. And that's a brick wall. That's a stone wall. I'm not going to get around that. I'm not going to get through it. And I'm too smart to beat my head against it. So I said, "Okay, thank you very much. I really appreciate it." And we get up and we leave. And we're getting into Lew's car, and so as we drive off he says, "Did you see what the old man was reading?"

I say, "No, why?"

"Screenplays."

So now I'm curious. Here's this guy, he lives in a hospital bed, and it's like a Raymond Chandler novel, this guy's in a fucking hospital bed in his living room and he's reading screenplays.

So I go home and I get out my *Encyclopedia of Film* and I look up this guy Everett Freeman. He had a thirty-year career in Hollywood. He's a writer-producer. And his first credit is *Larceny, Inc.*, Edward G. Robinson, '39 or '40, all the way up until the seventies. He created and wrote the *Glass Bottom Boat*, and he's in a hospital bed in his living room, smoking, and his kid's fourteen. I don't see them out in the backyard playing football a lot. So I can understand where this kid might have some interesting hobbies.

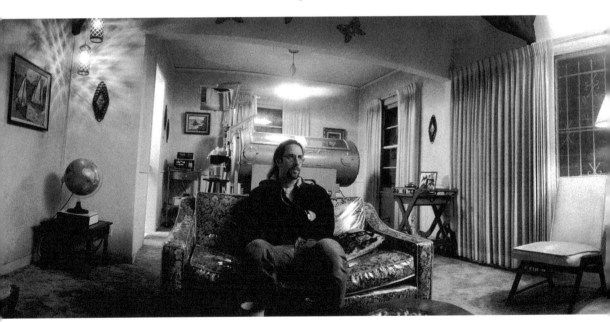

So back at the dinner party, there is another guy there who is very funny, and he started telling Lew stories, and we spent the whole night practically in Lewville. Just telling stories. And that was June of 1989. And then in 1992 I was talking to Joel, and he said, "Hey, I wrote a script about your buddy Lew. But we changed his name to Walter because we don't want to embarrass the guy. Do you want to read it?"

Well, I was very flattered. They had never asked me to read anything. So they sent me the script and I read it, *The Big Lebowski*. And I didn't get it. I thought the guy in the opening scene was Walter, the guy who was walking around in the grocery store and opening the carton of milk and tasting the milk and getting a little milk mustache and going up and writing the check for sixty-nine cents. I said, "Oh, this is Lew." And I forgot all about it. Until this guy told me he'd read a magazine article and the new Coen brothers movie is based entirely on my life.

And I still tell this story to my kids at USC. Which I think is absolutely pathetic. Over eight years ago. So now the kids at USC, they tell each other, "Oh, I'm taking a class from this guy that *The Big Lebowski* is based on." So these kids come into my class and they want to hear about how I'm the Dude. And I very carefully pass out this article and I say to them, "As you can see, Walter P. Sobchak is based on me, John Milius, and Lew." And the Dude is somebody completely different—that guy is Jeff Dowd.

But Joel and Ethan think I'm funny, a very funny guy. And one time they were in town and we were at dinner. And it was like January 1991. And we were kicking ass in Iraq. We'd bombed Iraq for about six months and then we attacked. Only it wasn't Iraq. It was Kuwait. And about forty thousand soldiers from the Iraq army surrendered.

Well, I felt embarrassed, you know, as a Vietnam veteran. As you recall, we lost that war. However, I do want you to know that when I left, we were winning. So I'm having dinner with Joel and Ethan, and I'm feeling kind of anxious and uneasy here, and I think I need to explain things to them, and I said, "All right, guys, you gotta understand. It's a lot easier to fight a war in the desert than it is to fight in *canopy jungle*."

Well, I thought we were going to have to call 911 and get oxygen for Joel. I thought he was going to hit the floor. He was laughing so hard. And so I get invited to the screening at the Writers' Guild and there is John Goodman, lacing up his bowling alley shoes, and he's talking to Jeff Bridges and he says, "Dude, you gotta understand, it's a lot easier to fight a war in the desert than it is in triple canopy." And I'm like, "What the fuck?" and I turn around and look at the doorway, and there is Joel. He's looking right at me. And laughing.

"I just rented *The Big Lebowski*, and I think those guys owe us money."

So I kind of milk this story. To this day, I'm still telling my classes. And one night I came home from class at USC, and my little phone-machine light is blinking—that little red blinking light—so I push the button and I get this message: "Listen, Exline, it's Lew. Lew from Texas. Listen, I didn't see this movie when it first came out. But I just rented *The Big Lebowski*, and I think those guys owe us money."

Bums: Do you have any idea what it is about the movie that resonates with people?

PE: I really think that it's just the humor. If anything, if I had to analyze it beyond the humor, it's the perfect adolescent movie because the Dude is a guy who just refuses to grow up, and the other Lebowski is like the nightmare father. Here's this guy who is just, like, doing what he wants to do, getting stoned and bowling and outsmarting the man. It's a movie that each viewing I notice something that's funny that I never noticed before. So in that way, it's kind of a gold mine.

Bums: Now, why do they call you "Uncle Pete"?

PE: The full title is "Uncle Pete, the Philosopher King of Hollywood." And at the beginning of our conversation I said that when I first met them, I was working for Mace Neufeld in Beverly Hills, a Hollywood producer.

Ethan is a philosophy major—he got a PhD or a master's from Princeton in philosophy. And I had dropped out of philosophy. I was trying to get a master's at Oregon, a PhD at Oregon, and he had every philosopher synthesized down to one line.

Socrates: "Can we know what it is? No, never."

Descartes: "This is what it is. It's this and not that."

And Aristotle says, "This is that and that is this."

And Kant: "The mind is a meat grinder and knowledge is a hamburger. Can you know if it's kosher? No, never."

And Ethan had a shitty job where no one had been able to last more than a week. It was typing columns of numbers for Macy's. And he'd had it for a year and a half. And nobody before him had ever lasted a week.

Now, I was a guy from Hollywood. I was a guy in a suit and tie. So they kinda figured I knew everything. I knew the business. I knew what was going on. And they were just cubs trying to figure it all out. So Ethan came up with Uncle Pete, the Philosopher King of Hollywood. It's the only thing I can figure.

Bums: Has your relationship to Vietnam changed? Is there a period when you were a bitter Vietnam vet? Or was that just all in humor?

PE: No. A former student of mine sent you the e-mail and told you that you can't have Lebowski Fest without Pete Exline, because the whole thing started with him. I did not pick up a chair. I did not throw it across the room. I kind of shoved it with my foot, which looks like I'm kicking it. And I use that joke every semester: "First Vietnam, now this chair!" And I use that joke every semester just like I use the joke, "Let me tell you one thing about Vietnam: We were winning when *I* left." That's just Ethan's exaggeration to amuse himself.

And the same with how it became a ratty little apartment and a shitty little rug. That's just Ethan changing things around to keep himself from falling asleep because he's so bored with, uh . . . the thing about Joel and Ethan is, once they make a movie, they don't want to ever talk about it again. And if you go up and say, "Wow, I really liked this," they're kind of like, "Yeah, well, that's over." So they obviously have terrific imaginations. You can look at their movies and see that they hardly ever imitate themselves. They hardly ever repeat things.

And they generally try to turn everything into a joke.

"BIG" LEW ABERNATHY: "We'll Brace the Kid. Should Be a Pushover."

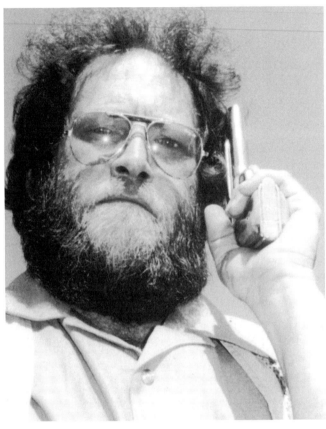

After Peter Exline told us of his friend whose idea it was to put the homework in a baggie and brace the twelve-year-old kid, we tracked him down and invited him to a Lebowski Fest. When he showed up in Austin, a fan rushed up to us and exclaimed, "Lew's here! He's cool as a kite, but I think he might be Amish." Upon further investigation we discovered that he was not, in fact, Amish, but that he's been just about everything else, including a private investigator (brother shamus), treasure hunter, screenwriter, and actor—his most notable role being one of the two submersible pilots in James Cameron's *Titanic*.

It is said that Big Lew is one-third of the inspiration for Walter (Exline plus Abernathy plus Milius, divided by John Goodman, equals Walter Sobchak). When Lew e-mailed his buddy James Cameron to let him know he was the guest of honor at Lebowski Fest, Cameron replied, "Congratulations! After thirty years in the film business, you are the inspiration for one-third of a fictional character."

Lew Abernathy: I finally get to set the record straight. I went to North Texas and studied philosophy and political science, then drifted to business. Ultimately I wound up in film.

And then after I left North Texas, I went out to California and I started going to USC. I went out to USC and got my master's in cinema.

USC is an expensive private school, and so my day job, or night job, was that I was a private investigator. That's how I paid for film school. I fell into it out of a lifelong search not to have a job. In this respect, I am the Dude. I'd rather coast.

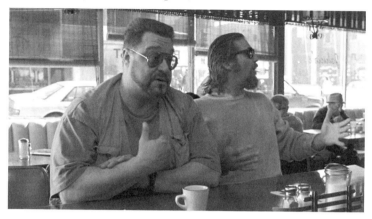

My firm was called L.A. Investigations, and I was a private investigator for fifteen years. When I met Peter Exline he was a studio executive at Universal, and Peter and I would hang out and have coffee in the morning, usually a place called Cafe 50's. Kindred spirits. We're both very much Walteresque: loud arguments and plenty of coffee.

So one day he calls me and says, "My car has been stolen."

So, okay, *And?* We *do* live in Los Angeles. So he says, "What do I do?"

I say, "Well, did you call the cops?"

He says, "Yeah, I called the cops and the insurance company."

And I said, "Well, you're done."

And he said, "Well, what happens?"

And I said, "Well, there are several scenarios. Either it got chopped and you'll never see it again; or it was used in the commission of a crime, in which case they'll find it but they'll hold it for twenty years as evidence; or they went on a joyride, which means they left it abandoned someplace, someone will tow it, and then a week or two later you'll get a card from the impound yard and you get the privilege of going down there and bailing your own car out. Because they charge you for towing *and* storage. More than the car is worth in a lot of cases. You see some real derelicts down at the impound yard."

So we go down to the impound yard and sure enough the car is there, and Peter is talking to the guy who runs the impound yard, who I guess is a policeman, but it seems to me is one rank up from dogcatcher.

So Peter is like, "Do you have any leads?" And the guy at the impound yard, to my

> **I had put some of the McDonald's wrappers in my briefcase. First of all, I had dusted them for prints.**

mind, is exactly like the guy in the movie. "Oh, yeah, leads, we got *tons* of leads. We got the whole force working on it!"

So while that was going on, I was checking out the car and telling Peter, "You know, it's not that bad." They busted out a gull window or maybe the rear window, and they tore up the transmission like idiots. They were clearly amateurs. And there were all these hamburger wrappers in there, literally dozens of them. They were just all over the car.

Bums: Sounds like a joyride situation.

LA: Yeah, it was. And so they'd gone to McDonald's, and I'm looking and there are these books, and it's like high school history, eighth-grade chemistry, or something. And I say, "Peter, are you going back to school?"

And he says, "What are you talking about?"

I said, "Are these *your* textbooks and *your* homework?" What was interesting was that the impound guy was giving the last of the zingers trying to prove to Peter that stolen cars are such a low priority and there is no way they can ever find these guys.

And so I whip out the homework and say, "Yeah, like maybe this guy? Start with this guy?" It was a pretty funny moment there.

And so we found the homework. And for whatever reason, Peter was on this real quest to try to set this kid on the straight and narrow.

He says, "I want to confront this kid."

And I say, "Bro, just turn it over to the cops and be done with it. You got your car back."

But he says, "No, I think I want to do this." It was like three or four days he debated it. So finally he contacted the boy's family, the mother or whatever.

I put on my best suit, what I called my court suit, just like Walter. And I had put some of the McDonald's wrappers in my briefcase. First of all, I had dusted them for prints. Not really—I hadn't lifted any prints, I just put the dust on there so that they'd show up, you know? And I put one in an evidence bag. And then I took the homework and I dusted it and I put it in an evidence bag, and so we drive over to this house in Westwood.

So we knock on the door and this really nice British lady, middle-aged, very proper, opens the door, and first of all, Peter hadn't told *her* I was coming, so immediately she's pissed off. That was a complete surprise to both of us. And of course she treats me like I've got leprosy.

We go in, and we go into the living room, and this is where the movie takes over, with the exception of the iron lung. The father has got IV bags and oxygen. He's very alert, he's watching us, he can tell what's going on. And behind him is a wall of screenplays and awards.

And I'm going, "Peter, what have you gotten me into?"

Bums: So, having gone to film school, did you recognize the name and know him?

LA: The thing was, we didn't know who he was. We didn't know who he was at first, but one look and I'd been in enough writers' homes to know that this guy is the real deal, he's a writer of some note.

Bums: Not exactly a lightweight.

LA: No. It was a nice house, a nice neighborhood, too, and the guy is just laying there and never says a word.

And we sit down and she brings the kid down. And that's when I basically did the Walter thing. I opened the briefcase—"Is this your homework, Larry? I've dusted it for prints, Larry, so don't lie!"

The kid said that he didn't steal the car, but he *was* riding in it. And so I said, "Well, I'll give you a choice." I said, "You need to do one of two things. You can either tell me who was in the car, or you can tell the police. But we're gonna find out who stole the car. And right now you're our best lead."

And so he's looking over at his mother, and she says, "Can we have twenty-four hours to think about it and discuss it?"

He has health problems

The Iron Lung was invented by Philip Drinker and Agassiz Shaw of Harvard Medical School and used primarily during the polio epidemic of the 1940s and 1950s.

And I say, "Sure. It's the weekend. I'll wait till Monday." And then I kind of gave some tired old speech. Peter did the talking at first, but Peter was insane. Babbling on and not making any sense. And I'm trying to get to the point so that we can get the hell out of there.

Bums: "Dude, please. *I'll* handle this."

LA: [*laughing*] Yeah, right. "You're killing your father, Larry." No, but what I did say, because I'd seen his homework, was, "You need to spend more time with your homework and less time joyriding with your friends. Because let me tell you something, it looks here like you're just a half-assed student, but you're a fucking *lousy* criminal, kid. You need to give up the crime aspect of this right now."

What was really weird was I don't think any of us—me, Peter, the mother, or the son—mentioned that there was this dying man in our midst. It was kind of like we all just didn't say anything about him.

That was pretty much the end of it for me, thank God. But I was always curious, because there were a couple of other things that happened to me as a private investigator. I was working a case in Malibu, which, as you can imagine, is like rich hillbillies. It's very incestuous, nepotistic. I was working a case where I had to watch some people, and they called the cops on me, even though I was in a public place.

Bums: They knew that you were surveilling this person?

LA: Yeah, they pinched me. I got busted. I was probably trying to dress up like a surfer or something. So they dragged me in to the sheriff, and he said, "What are you doing?" And I said, "I'm working a case."

He wanted to know all the specific details, and I told him to go fuck himself, and he bounced a coffee cup off my head and threw me out of town. And the cup broke when it hit my head.

Bums: Did you call him anything?

LA: I think I might've said something ugly. And he did say something about, "I don't like your face, I don't like you . . ." He had a whole speech, and you can tell it was a stupid speech that he gave to other people, this canned speech. The guy was coming off like he was freakin' Kojak. And he did use those immortal words, "Stay out of my beach community!"

Bums: What was the time frame on this sheriff story?

LA: That would have been mid-eighties.

And then the other thing was the scattering of the ashes off the ocean view. Apparently this is something that happens every six months like clockwork. Dipshits go up there and try to scatter their ashes into the wind. And when I was at USC, a film student got killed in a motorcycle accident. He didn't have any family, and it was kind of up to us to bury him. But we didn't use a coffee can. We had him in a baggie. And his girlfriend was there too. And two guys were trying to scatter the ashes into the wind—which is stupid—and it all blew back on all of us.

But the thing about it was that the guy was still partially in the bag, and it had kind of gotten wet, so it's kind of pasty, and it was really a disaster. And we're all just covered with this guy. And finally, at the last minute, he shakes out the last little bit—and this is before they started using grinders, apparently—and a chunk of bone about that big [*makes size of a quarter*] bounced out and landed right at his girlfriend's feet. And she just passed the fuck out right there.

> # I'm sitting there watching this movie, and it starts to become eerily familiar.

I was standing there going, "Okay, well, this is *not* what I want my funeral to be like." But the thing about it is that my understanding is that that particular scene has played itself out at various locations up and down the coast since time immemorial.

Then I worked this case one time where it was marital infidelity. It was stupid—rich people, they were insane—and the house I went to, it was so much like *Sunset Boulevard*. You go to the creepy old house, and you knew it used to be *somebody's* house, but it was a little bit in disrepair.

And so I ring the doorbell, and the butler or manservant says, "Mrs. So-and-so is back here." And so he leads me through this house, which is clearly big money. But it looks like no one has even lived in the house for a while. And then he leads me out back to the guesthouse, but halfway there he stops and says, "Through there." Like Brandt. "In seclusion."

So I knock on the door and say, "Helloooo?" And it sounds like people are boning—I hear this *fuh hah boom boom boom*. And I'm knocking on the door, and I open it a little bit because it's not shut, and it's a woman on a bungee cord making body prints on the floor. It's bizarre. She had paint all over the place and was butt naked—except for the little bungee-cord thing.

And then she stops bouncing there and says, "One moment, Mr. Abernathy, I'll be right with you." She put on a robe, and we sat down and had a business meeting. Bizarre. It never became anything.

Bums: So you hadn't heard anything during *Lebowski* production about these stories serving as inspirations?

LA: No. I knew nothing about the movie whatsoever. All I knew is the Coen brothers had come out with a new movie and it had tanked. But somebody had said, "It's funny and you should watch it." Someone recommended it who had no idea of my involvement on any level.

So I'm sitting there watching this movie, and it starts to become eerily familiar. And I'm sitting there going, "Did I read this script at some point? Or worse yet, did they hire me to punch this thing up? Did I work for the Coen brothers and I don't remember it?" Of course, I'm staring at the joint and I'm thinking, "Damn! I think I'm losing my mind!"

And I think finally, when they got to Little Larry Sellers's house, I finally thought, "This is *très* fucked up. This is my life. My life is in a movie and I don't know how." And of course I got to thinking about it, and being a former detective I said, "This stinks of Exline." So I called up Peter, which I actually think might be the last time I spoke to him, and asked him what the hell happened.

JAIK FREEMAN: The Real Little Larry

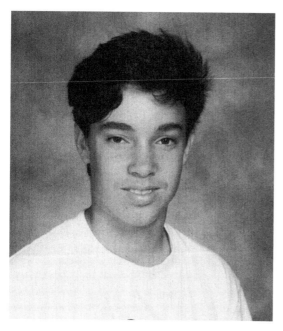

One of our biggest thrills in assembling this book was locating and interviewing the real Little Larry. As it turns out, he's neither a brat nor a criminal. He's a pretty funny, well-adjusted dude. Now thirty-two, Jaik followed his father, the famous writer Everett Freeman, into the film business. And until we called, he had no idea that the day in his living room when two strange men arrived with his homework in a baggie had been a pivotal inspiration for *The Big Lebowski*. Here is his story. All this took place in 1986–1987. He was in seventh grade at the time.

Bums: As we told you, we've actually spoken to the guys who came to your house that day.

Jaik Freeman: Right.

Bums: And got *their* version of the story.

JF: I've got some questions for you. I've got some questions about what actually happened that day. As opposed to what's gone down in the movie.

Bums: Yeah, that's what we want to get to the bottom of. But before you tell us that story, we're curious what your reaction has been this week since we left you that phone message and first spoke with you. Was it your mom that we had left a message with initially?

JF: Yeah, that was my mother. My father—I know you asked for my father on the answering machine, but he passed away years ago, actually.

So, yeah, you know, I wasn't too thrilled by the portrayal. Especially because I didn't steal the car.

Bums: But what did your mom say to you about the phone message?

JF: Honestly, she just asked, "Do you know anything about this?" And I went over to the house, listened to the message, and I obviously had *no* idea what you were talking about. She didn't either.

She had been in the room, she took the phone call from these guys, and then was there sitting next to my father, who was there in the room with us at the time—you know, smoking furiously—but she honestly didn't *really* remember it. It was twenty years ago and it was right before my father passed away, and he was really ill at that time.

> **And as I recall, he opened up the briefcase and said, "Is this your homework?" That part was exactly like in the movie. It was in this little plastic wrapper.**

Bums: So when we talked with you initially and explained it to you, you had no idea that this incident had inspired this scene from the film?

JF: No, none at all. And I had you on speakerphone, and my girlfriend was sitting there, and you were describing the scene, and she was nodding her head furiously, like, "*I know the scene! I know the scene!*" and I'm thinking to myself, Well, that sounds familiar, but I don't remember it from the movie.

Bums: Did you go out and rent the movie after that conversation?

JF: I did. I rented it over the weekend.

Bums: And you had seen it before, right?

JF: I *had*, but it had been so long ago, and I don't really have much time these days to really hang out and watch TV or watch movies.

Bums: So you said it was twenty years ago?

JF: Yeah, I was twelve.

Bums: Do you remember what you were doing when your mom called you down when the doorbell rang?

JF: Well, I vaguely remember her saying, "Well, what's going on?" And asking me if I'd stolen a car. And I just said, *"No."* And she said, "Well, these guys are coming over." And she is in panic mode at this point, or ready to kill me for something that I haven't done.

And so the guy comes over, and I remember him walking through the door. The guy who was with him, I remember what he was wearing, but I don't remember his face. He was in a white shirt, with a black or a dark tie and some slacks. You know, was he *actually* a private investigator, or was he just his friend pretending to be a private investigator?

Bums: No, he was actually a private investigator. The big guy. His name is Lew Abernathy, and he says hi, by the way. And "No hard feelings."

JF: Lew Abernathy. Okay. I had *no* idea what to make of this guy, because—I mean, I knew who stole the car, and you're going to hear about this—but I was just thinking, Well, why is *he* here? And why aren't the police here? I mean, who is this guy? I'm twelve years old, and I'm feeling like, What am I dealing with here?

So that was my take on the guy, the guy that he brought over with him, the private investigator. And as for the guy who owned the car, he was just kind of sitting there with this scowl on his face the whole time, just kind of staring me down.

Bums: So do you remember anything about the briefcase?

JF: Okay, my father *was* confined to a hospital bed in the living room. Like I said, he was paralyzed on his left side and it was a hard time, and he died about four years after that. So he was in the hospital bed.

The couch was facing the bed, and they were on the couch. My mother was in a chair next to the couch, and I was situated in a chair at the base of the hospital bed, looking at them and my mother. It was kind of like in the round—*kind of.*

And I remember them asking me, "Did you steal this car?" And I said, *"No."* [*flatly and finally, like a stonewalling teenager*].

So he drops his briefcase on the table, and he says, "Are you *sure?*"

And I said, "Yeah."

And as I recall, he opened up the briefcase and said, "Is this your homework?" That part was exactly like in the movie. It was in this little plastic wrapper.

And so I say, "Yeah, that's my homework." [*flippantly*]

And it was a *math* book, *not* history—if that makes any difference. It was my algebra book. And my algebra book had been left in the car. And my homework was obviously left in the book. And that's basically how they got me.

So I said, "Yeah, that's my homework."

And then they said, "Well, there were McDonald's wrappers in the car, and with that kind of greasy stuff, there'll be fingerprints everywhere."

And I was like, *"Great!* Fingerprint the car!"

So they are sitting there kind of scowling at me, and finally I remember saying to them, "Look, I don't know either of you guys, and I'm not going to say anything else. If you take me down to the police station, I'd be more than happy to file a police report. But I'm not going to say anything else here."

And after that, there was nothing else that came out. Honestly, I figured that what happened was that they *did* go down, they *did* fingerprint the car, they *didn't* find my fingerprints, and *that's* why I never heard from them again.

The way the car got stolen, I guess, is Harry Jones.* Harry Jones was a friend of mine at that point. He was a couple of years older than me—most of my friends were a couple years older than me. My best friend lived directly behind me on the other side of the block, and he was two years older than me. And I kinda hung out with all the kids in his grade. So, you know, I was twelve years old, hanging out with all the older kids.

So Harry Jones had stolen the car. And he actually a little later on got busted for a *string* of stolen cars. If I remember correctly, this guy's car was a Toyota. I think it was a Corolla or something. Because Harry had told everybody that you could get into these cars very easily simply with a screwdriver and a pair of vise grips. All you had to do was break the window, and then you could just slam the screwdriver into the ignition, crack the ignition. So that was why, I guess, his car got targeted.

---

* This name and others in the book have been changed to protect the privacy of individuals. This is a private residence, man!

Harry had borrowed my math book. He'd said, "I need to borrow your math book," and I'd just said, "Okay. Sure, no problem." I'd done *my* homework. And it didn't really dawn on me why he'd want to borrow *mine*, because—I thought about this later on—he was in a higher grade than me, so if he wanted to show up in class with a book . . . whatever.

So I'd loaned him my book and he, I guess, had left it in the car. And go figure. I'm the guy that gets immortalized as a dunce in the movie.

Bums: Would you say that you were more annoyed and pissed, or were you scared of these people—this crazy dude waving this homework in your face?

JF: I wasn't scared of him. At that point, I was scared because what do your parents think when this happens? And you honestly haven't done it. Of all the fuck-ups that I've made in my life, you know, like, "I didn't do this."

Like I said, my father was sick at that time, so that was really more my concern. Who are these guys to come in here waving this shit around in my face when they obviously haven't done *their* fucking homework?

Bums: When you saw the movie, you didn't have any sort of air of familiarity—it didn't seem eerily familiar or anything?

JF: Oh, yeah, definitely when I saw it again. I mean obviously they pretty substantially exaggerated what my father was like. It was like he was hooked up to some respirator in a 1950s sci-fi machine, you know. And there was no maid, by the way.

Bums: No Pilar. Now, they claim that your dad was actually reading some screenplays. Was he a screenwriter?

JF: Oh, yeah. That's also true. My father was a writer-producer for years. Sam Goldwyn brought him out to Hollywood in the thirties or something—I think it was '37, or it might be later than that—and he worked in TV, he worked in film. Got two Oscar nods. Everett Freeman.

Bums: Now, did this meeting have an impact on you? Did you straighten up?

JF: [*offended*] Did this meeting have any effect on me? Was I scared straight by some joker and a guy pretending to be a private investigator? Or a private investigator pretending to be someone important?

No. That didn't scare me straight. I mean, after that it was teenage rebellion. My father died and it was teenage rebellion, and I acted out for a number of years and slowly but surely straightened myself out, and now I make the world a better place. That's a joke, by the way.

Bums: Do you feel like maybe the Coen brothers owe you anything?

JF: *They owe me big.* And they don't even know it yet.

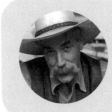

The Stranger Says . . .

"Good night, sweet prince." On August 7, 2002, Hollywood Star Lanes in Los Angeles, where much of the film was shot, closed to make way for an elementary school.

JOHN MILIUS: An Inspiration for Walter. He's Not Housebroken.

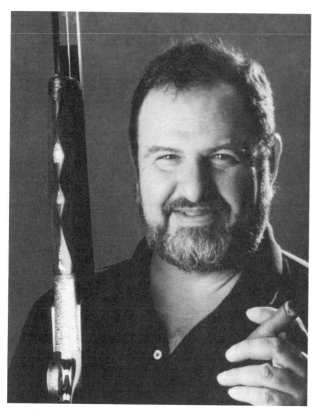

The character of Walter Sobchak was largely based on Hollywood legend John Milius. Milius wrote *Apocalypse Now* and wrote and directed *Big Wednesday*, *Conan the Barbarian*, and *Red Dawn*, among many, many others. Along with his film credits, he's known throughout Hollywood as a maverick, a militarist, and a political conservative in a town famous for its left-leaning politics. (As he himself puts it, "I'm not housebroken.") For many years a large photograph of an atom bomb exploding over the Bikini Islands occupied the wall behind his desk. And let's also not forget—let's not forget, Dude—that he is one of the founders of a little enterprise called the Ultimate Fighting Championship. Not exactly a lightweight.

John Milius: Everybody loves *The Big Lebowski*. My kids love that movie. They all say, "That's our father, there! That's him!" They like that better than any of *my* movies.

Bums: How did you meet the Coen brothers?

JM: Well, I saw their movies. And I'm not positive, but I think they just called me up out of the blue and they wanted me to act in a movie for them.

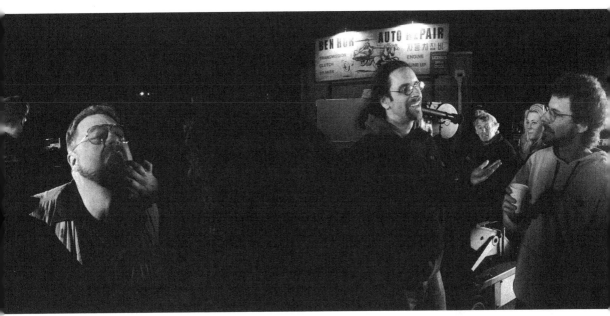

They wanted me to be the head of the studio in *Barton Fink*. And the guy got an Oscar nomination for doing that, Michael Lerner. And I read it, and I remember I said, "This is *real acting*!" It's like paragraphs of lines and stuff like this, and I said, "You know, I can't do this. I'll crack on the day. I'll get up there and I'll just freeze up. I can walk by and smirk or say a couple of words, but I can't do this, you know? This is the real stuff!" So they were very disappointed that I didn't do that.

Bums: At what point did you realize that you were part of the inspiration for Walter?

JM: Well, they never told me. But people who saw the movie said, "That's you!" And of course I looked at the movie, and I said, "Yes, it is!" I especially like where Walter bites the guy's ear off.

The first time I saw the movie, I just laughed and laughed. Most of the time when people do an imitation of you, you're embarrassed and it's awful. You say, "Oh, I don't really sound like that. I'm not really like this." This is one where I just sat there and *cracked up*. It was like the best kind of roast.

Bums: So what character traits would you say that you and Walter have in common?

JM: Well, I don't bowl. Like he says, "I don't roll on Shabbos!" I just love that whole idea of that guy, you know, that he's Jewish when it's convenient. He's constantly bringing the Vietnam War into anything. And the ending is so ludicrous. They're dumping the ashes into the ocean, and he starts talking about those who were lost at Khe Sanh and such and such. And the Dude says, "What the fuck does that have to do with anything?"

And he really didn't have an answer. You know, like, "Why not? Why doesn't Vietnam have anything to do with it? It has to do with everything!" What I love about the character is he has such great enthusiasm. The whole movie is so good. The Dude is just a wonderful character too.

There are certain movies that, as time goes on, they acquire more and more weight and importance, and that's one of them. And the movies that people think are very important at the time often are not important at all as time goes on.

Bums: Why do you think that is? What is it about this movie?

JM: I don't know. It really is something you remember, and it makes you feel good. It just has something that touches you, you know, that is just outrageous. It's funny because it really has a greater timelessness than their other movies, doesn't it? And they've made some good movies.

Bums: Off the top of your head, do you have a favorite scene from the movie?

JM: Oh, I don't know. Like I said, I love the final action confrontation between those guys. Because you're waiting for that the whole movie. And it really makes you want to cheer,

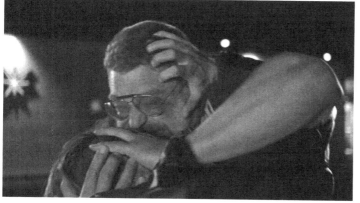

you know? There's just something about it, it just really makes you feel good. You want to cheer. And that doesn't work usually in movies.

But there are movies that have that effect that are kind of plain. When I talk about a comedy, I always talk about a *Caddyshack*-grade comedy, because most comedies aren't. Most comedies, a couple of years later you say, "That wasn't so funny." But some of these movies gather impetus and weight.

And you never know what that's going to be. *Viva Las Vegas* has that quality to it. If you want to have a good night at your big-screen TV, get *Viva Las Vegas*. Elvis, Ann-Margaret, in Las Vegas. *Hard to beat.*

> **I especially like where Walter bites the guy's ear off.**

But there are a lot of films that are so important and such great films that don't mean a thing later, you know? Like most of the *Star Wars* movies, to me, can be used for interrogational purposes. I mean, this is one of only a handful of modern movies that are worthy of a book.

Bums: Well, we'd also like to switch gears from the movie and ask you a few things about yourself. What's it like to be a conservative in Hollywood?

JM: You know, I'm not a standard conservative. See, I like to call myself a Zen anarchist.

Bums: What does that mean?

JM: It means I can do whatever I want! Right now I'm very angry with the Republican Party because of their support of corporate greed. Which I think is even worse than terrorism. And you start talking about these guys like Ken Lay and Skilling and I turn into a Maoist, you know? I want show trials with tumbrels with these guys in them and signs around their necks. Public executions, public denunciations, things like that. Where they are actually shot and charged for the bullets—their families are charged for the bullets.

I mean, see, I really actually believe that stuff. I just hate it. But at the same time I'm a militarist, you know? So I don't really make a lot of sense. I often think about when David Bowie was once told by a journalist, "You've contradicted yourself several times, Mr. Bowie." And he said, "Well, I'm a *rock star.*" That's how I look at it.

But being a conservative—I'm everything that they don't like in Hollywood. An agent once said that the problem with Hollywood is that there are still rattlesnakes in Bel Air and Milius is there. They blacklisted me and cut me out of the last ten years or fifteen years. So it's been pretty rough. But I'm amazed how much I actually got done. And I'm still at large, still doing stuff. I did *Rome*. And I'm doing stuff right now.

So the fact that I'm still out there, that I've watched all the studio executives who snubbed me fall into decay and be savagely attacked by their own friends—I often like to say, "I'm the Yeti." That was my surfing name. They haven't caught me yet!

Bums: How did you become a militarist? We read that you weren't able to serve in the military, although you wanted to.

JM: Yeah, I was really, really disgusted with my life and myself. And I probably have chafed at that ever since. I probably feel that I didn't get my chance to get killed in Vietnam. I mean, it's really stupid to take that attitude, but still. And so I just felt very supportive of the military and did everything I did to support the military and go off to whatever wars we had. But I haven't been to Baghdad. I'm too slow now. I'd probably get somebody killed.

Bums: Now, is it true that you were one of the original founders of the Ultimate Fighting Championship?

JM: Absolutely. I remember when I did that, and they had the second one, and Harrison Ford—we were making *Clear and Present Danger* then—he said, "Do you know what you brought about? You've brought about gladiatorial combat!" And I said, "Right on!"

And it's gotten bigger than ever. I think it's going to overtake boxing. Because I think people really want that. I think people really want to get down to being honest about it, you know? On YouTube they watch the Iraqi War. They say, "Why do I want to go see a war movie when I can see people blown up?"

Our society is really changing. We need stronger dope, you know what I mean? We require a bigger thrill. The idea of having boxing—it's been there, it's happened. UFC is gladiatorial, and people want that. You watch, it'll change.

Bums: What did the Coens see in you that they were able to transform into Walter?

JM: Well, I'm not your normal, run-of-the-mill character out there, you know? I have some pretty crazy attitudes. And I also—I'm not completely housebroken. They sort of liked that. The thing that's interesting about Hollywood today is that it's a town of lots of people working who are motivated by fear. And there is this terrible cloud of fear that hangs over everything. Everything is done with fear. The whole purpose and structure is about fear. You're afraid you'll get fired if you do something wrong. You make a movie that isn't good enough, doesn't make enough money on opening weekend, you'll never make another movie. This kind of thing. And so people like me don't exist.

Bums: Too dangerous?

JM: Yeah, the only guy who is kind of like me is Quentin Tarantino. Whereas people like me were quite common in the old Hollywood. Mitchum was that way. John Huston was that way. Mitchum did whatever he wanted. People just accepted him because he was Mitchum. Steve McQueen was that way. Steve McQueen was not housebroken. But he didn't make a big deal of it, you know? He was just that way.

Peckinpah was probably the most extreme. But one of the things about Peckinpah that was really great was that he believed in what he was doing. He wasn't scared of anything. He was a zealot, you know? And so you had to have respect for him. He didn't play the game by their rules. He didn't sit there and say, "Okay, I'm going to be really clever and smart." There was nothing clever at all about them. They just did what they did.

That is gone from our society. And really we need that. We need that kind of thing.

CHAPTER FOUR

ARE WE ALONE?
OR, HOW *THE BIG LEBOWSKI* BECAME A CULT CLASSIC

Each year, billions and billions of films are produced and distributed to theaters, living rooms, and street vendors throughout the world. And among those, if just one in every million were produced without the mainstream audience in mind, and just one in every million of those films had the ability to sustain the attention of some unsuspecting viewer late at night, and just one in every million of those viewers were the type of person to snub *Pearl Harbor*, then there would literally be millions and millions of cult movie fans out there, shaking their fists at the mainstream, white-noise, money-making machines.

No, my friend, we are not alone.

And since we are few, but not alone, it is our job, our duty, to reach out to each other and make contact with our fellow fandom friends. We must join forces and, through

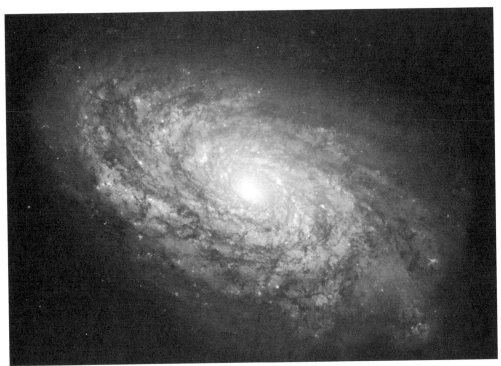

numbers and our influence on DVD sales, let it be known that we, the brotherhood of cult movie fans, are discontent as hell, and we're not going to . . . hey, was that *Goonies*? Go back. Pass the popcorn.

Where were we? Oh, yeah, money-making machines, or marketing them, or the lack thereof. Take for instance the tagline . . .

Times Like These Call for a Big Lebowski?

Look at any of the original posters from *The Big Lebowski*'s theatrical release, and that's the tagline you'll find. Not "Mark It 8, Dude." Not "The Dude Abides." Not "The Story Is Ludicrous," or any of the movie's other gems. But "Times Like These Call for a Big Lebowski." In terms of capturing the movie's essence, you couldn't do much worse.

But if you did go looking for worse—say, if your curiosity got the best of you and you couldn't help but wonder, "If there was a worse way to pitch *The Big Lebowski*, what would it be?"—you would actually be in luck. You wouldn't need to look any further than the case from the movie's original DVD release, which stated that the Dude's "carpet" really "made the room hang together."

> The Dude. One cool guy. Who one day comes home to find two thugs have broken in and ruined his favorite carpet - the one that made the room "hang together." Thing is, they did it because he's got the exact same name as one of the richest men in town, Lebowski. But, hey, no problem, he'll get even. At least he'll get someone to pay for a new carpet.

Fuckin' amateurs.

As is widely known throughout the Lebowski galaxy, the Dude's rug really *tied* the room together. If you're not yet a huge fan of the movie, you're probably muttering, "What's the big deal?" But that's the point. To true Achievers, that's the equivalent of quoting Darth Vader as saying, "Luke, I am your mother."

Looking back, though, it's understandable that they missed the mark. Here you had a movie that was referencing and reshaping noir classics like *The Big Sleep* and *The Long Goodbye* without being obvious about it. The Coen brothers took the plot of a hard-boiled, Chandleresque crime caper but replaced the sure-footed, ball-swinging private investigator who would normally star in such a movie with a lovable, jellies-wearing stoner. They buddied him up with a hotheaded Vietnam vet and set them loose to bicker like an old married couple. There were no exploding helicopters, no epic battle scenes. Just a '73 Torino, a bag of dirty undies, and a severed toe.

Add to that the fact that *The Big Lebowski* was released on the heels of *Fargo*, which had become an unlikely financial hit: It had earned two Oscars and helped certify the Coen brothers as more than fringe auteurs. The pressure was on for *The Big Lebowski* to enjoy the same kind of success, and the studio was looking for some way—any way—to help it connect with a mainstream audience.

And so the studio did what any Marketing 101 textbook will tell you to do. They came up with the least abrasive, most consumer-friendly tag they could muster: "Times Like These Call for a Big Lebowski."

But if the people responsible for marketing *The Big Lebowski* didn't seem to get the movie's true appeal, they weren't alone. Most of the people who went to see it in the theater didn't get it, either. Released on March 6, 1998, *The Big Lebowski* ambled out of the gates, pulling in just over $5 million at the box office its opening weekend. That put it well behind the weekend's other big openers—*U.S. Marshals*, *Twilight*, and *Hush* (all part of your DVD collection, right?)—and still further behind *Titanic*, which sucked down $20 million in its twelfth week of release. Dismissed by many critics as a forgettable mess, *The Big Lebowski* would go on to barely earn back its $15 million budget at the theaters, pulling in much less than *Fargo* even though it cost twice as much to make and played on more screens.

Although few (if any) people realized it at the time, in disappearing so quickly from theaters, *The Big Lebowski* had actually vanished down a rabbit hole that would eventually deliver it into the underground world of cult phenomena.

That, and a Pair of Testicles

What makes a cult movie, Mr. Lebowski? We didn't know, sir. But we did have an Internet connection and a healthy ability to suspend disbelief.

A little digging uncovered the idea that the cult phenomenon is as old as humanity itself. Recent studies of cave drawings, for example, have demonstrated that they were actually crafted as part of stage plays put on at midnight by cavemen in fishnet stockings . . . and then there's the Bible—who saw that one coming? And then three thousand years of beautiful tradition, from Stonehenge to crop circles, tattoos to ironic haircuts . . . the list is virtually endless.

Applied specifically to film, the idea of a cult movie entered the parlance of our times in the late 1960s. A time warp back to that era reveals the concept being used both as a term of appreciation for older movies like *Casablanca* and *Citizen Kane*, the staples of art houses, and as a term of respect for newer movies like *El Topo* and *Pink Flamingoes* that were too weird or disturbing for your average Brad and Janet but were adored by a fanatical minority.

The publication of Danny Peary's book *Cult Movies* in 1981 gave the movement a clearer definition.* A collection of the top one hundred cult films at the time, the book included a foreword that described the cult-movie phenomenon in a way that has yet to be surpassed: "The typical Hollywood product has little potential for becoming a cult favorite because it is perceived by everyone in basically the same way . . . On the other hand, cult films are born in controversy . . . Cultists believe they are among the blessed few who have discovered something in particular films that the average moviegoer and critic have missed—the something that makes the pictures extraordinary."

Peary went on to describe the unique way in which movies come to achieve cult status: "While word of mouth certainly plays a large part in the growth of cults for individual films, what is fascinating is that *in the beginning* pockets of people will embrace a film they have heard nothing about while clear across the country others independently will react identically to the same picture. There is nothing more exciting than discovering you

---

* Peary, Danny. *Cult Movies*. New York: Gramercy Books, 1981.

are not the only person obsessed with a picture critics hate, the public stays away from en masse, and film texts ignore."

Discovering that passage, we felt as if new shit had not just come to light but smacked us in the forehead. Placed in that context, *The Big Lebowski*'s indifferent performance at the box office was not really a failure at all. It was an essential ingredient to its later success.

At the same time, it was stupefying to realize that what we'd been experiencing the past few years was actually part of a larger phenomenon that had been repeated numerous times over the past few decades.

Shut the Fuck Up, Donny!

To begin with, "clear across the country," others were, in fact, reacting in just the same way that we were. In July of 2002, at almost exactly the same time that we hatched the idea for Lebowski Fest at the tattoo convention in Louisville, Santa Cruz–based Steve Palopoli was the first journalist to recognize in print *The Big Lebowski*'s burgeoning cult status. Although we didn't learn of it until a year later, he wrote an article for *Metro Santa Cruz* describing a growing base of fanatical Lebowski fans that was beginning to connect with itself.

When we caught up with Palopoli by phone, he talked about seeing *The Big Lebowski* when it first came out in the theaters, and then a few times on video, but he said that it wasn't until he attended a midnight screening in 2000 at the New Beverly Cinema in L.A. that he glimpsed what was beginning to happen. "Suddenly it was like I was connecting with Lebowski fans in all sorts of unlikely places. And 'Shut the fuck up, Donny!' was the gateway quote. You'd say, 'Shut the fuck up, Donny!' as part of your conversation, and the other person would look surprised and say, '*Lebowski!* Shut the fuck up, Donny!' and there would be this instant bond. And it was exciting because it was so random."

Two years later he'd moved to Santa Cruz and begun writing for a paper there. The article that he eventually dedicated to *The Big Lebowski* was originally meant to focus on the musician Robert Earl Keen. He loved Keen but had written about him several times before and wanted a new angle. While talking to a musician about *The Big Lebowski* (which by then had become a not-unusual occurrence), he discovered that Keen watched the movie all the time and quoted it on his tour bus. During his interview with Keen he asked about *The Big Lebowski*, and Keen did it, too—the same gateway quote, "*Lebowski!*

Shut the fuck up, Donny!" After trading a few quotes, Keen said, "You should really talk to my bassist, Bill Whitbeck. He's watched it well over a hundred times. He wants someone at his funeral to give the Donny eulogy—and his name isn't even Donny!"

With such an entertainingly fanatical fan to use as a hook, Palopoli took his chance to write a Lebowski article and vent about his own love for the movie. The response amazed him: letter after letter from people telling him how much they loved *Lebowski*, and how great it was to know they weren't alone.

Not long after Palopoli's article came out, the programmer for the local midnight movie series in Santa Cruz decided to run *The Big Lebowski*. "The first weekend they played it, they turned away several hundred people," Palopoli said. "They held it over, which they had never done, for six weeks. It was like an old-fashioned movie experience. People were yelling quotes before it even started. It sold out every weekend for a month."

And We Do Enter the Next Round-Robin

In his article, Palopoli went beyond just describing *The Big Lebowski*'s growing popularity. He also explained that what made *The Big Lebowski*'s cult popularity so surprising was that it came at a time when cult movies as a whole were floundering. He detailed how the growing success of a few cult movies led to a chain reaction over the next two decades in which "cult movies became so cool (and such potential cash cows in the profit-recycling world of home video) that every studio wanted one." Meanwhile the introduction of video rentals, cable, and the Internet allowed mainstream audiences to become increasingly more tuned in to life on the fringe so that "offbeat movies like . . . *The Blair Witch Project*, which once would have been relegated to cultdom, became massive, overhyped hits." With studios clamoring to cash in, and audiences seeming increasingly receptive, it was only a matter of time before we were flooded with "ready-made weirdness like *Liquid Sky* or camp like *Sorority Babes in the Slimeball Bowl-O-Rama*, all of them so self-aware of their cult potential they made you wince."

By the late nineties, this had all proceeded to backfire quite nicely. Studios began to realize that cult movies were no longer the gravy train with biscuit wheels they had once hoped for. Audiences, justifiably jaded, adopted an attitude of, "Fool me once, shame on you. Fool me twice, you . . . you . . . you won't fool me again."

Zat's Why Zay Sent Me . . . I Um Exphurt

"Joel and Ethan did not make *The Big Lebowski* with the intention of making a cult film."

That voice of familiarity and authority, believe it or not, does not belong to us. Like Bunny with her broken cable, we realized we had reached the limits of our resources and decided to call in *ze exphurt*.

And so, graciously if a little grudgingly (as if a university professor had been asked to substitute-teach seventh grade), Ben Barenholtz agreed to help us clarify the cult-movie phenomenon and *The Big Lebowski*'s place within it.

A film-industry legend with a career spanning more than forty years, Barenholtz not only originated the midnight-movie format at his Elgin Theater in New York City in the early 1970s; he also spotted the originality and potential of the Coen brothers' first film, *Blood Simple*, and produced their first three pictures.

"The one element about a cult movie," he goes on, "is that you cannot intentionally create a cult movie or a midnight movie. You cannot start out with that intention. Those things are created by the audience."

The first movie that Barenholtz played at midnight at the Elgin Theater was *El Topo* in January 1971. "I convinced [the filmmakers] to open it at midnight without advertising, strictly through word of mouth, because I knew that in wide release it would've lasted about a week. I ran it seven nights a week, and by the second week we were selling out six hundred seats by word of mouth. I would not screen it for critics. It ran for six months that way, and then John Lennon saw it and decided he wanted to buy the film. And they bought the film and opened it in wide release. I remember seeing a huge ALAN KLEIN PRESENTS EL TOPO sign in Times Square—Alan Klein was their manager—and it did last about a week. And they were so embarrassed that they didn't show it again for years."

Barenholtz continues with stories of *Pink Flamingoes*, *Eraserhead*, *The Harder They Come*, and *Night of the Living Dead*, an essential history of cult movies from their birth to the present, delivered in the space of a few breaths.

"All of these films, they are really all different," he sums up. "They are not cookie-cutter films. Also, I think when you look at those films in retrospect, they also very much reflect their times and what their audience is into at that time. I realized that if *El Topo* had opened ten years later, it wouldn't have lasted a day. The element of timing is huge with these kinds of films, and each one is different."

Crazy as it seemed, what he was saying was that *The Big Lebowski*'s marketing machine had it right all along: Times like these really *did* call for a Big Lebowski.

"In that kind of film, the people you have to talk to are the ones who are seeing it ten times or twenty times. They are more the definition of the cult film. It's the audience that does it."

We couldn't agree more. And so we've devoted the next chapter to *The Big Lebowski*'s fans—to looking at why they're so devoted to the film, but also to giving them the credit they're due.

And we're talkin' about the Achievers here. Sometimes there's a fan who . . . well, they're the fan for their time 'n' place. They fit right in there.

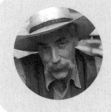

The Stranger Says . . .

"The ringer cannot look empty." The ringer toss was filmed in reverse so that they could get the arc just right.

CHAPTER FIVE

THE ACHIEVERS. AND PROUD WE ARE OF ALL OF THEM

achiev·er *n* **1** somebody who succeeds in doing or gaining a particular thing **2** inner-city children of promise, but without the necessary means for a necessary means for a higher education **3** the preferred nomenclature for a fan of *The Big Lebowski*

am·a·teur *n* **1** one who has only limited skill in, or knowledge of, an activity **2** one who simply doesn't "get" *The Big Lebowski* or why anyone in their right mind would wear a bathrobe to a bowling alley and drink several White Russians with hundreds of other equally zealous fans *note*: The word *fucking* can precede the term to add emphasis <What a fucking ~!> **antonym = achiever**

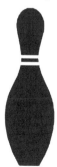

This is a fan book—written by the fans, for the fans. The following are interviews with fans from around the world. Some you may have heard of, some you may have not. The one thing we all share: We love this fucking movie.

PATTON OSWALT—Los Angeles

Name: Patton Oswalt

Residence: Los Angeles

Are you employed? Comedian, actor (*Magnolia*, *King of Queens*), writer (*Mad TV*, HBO, *Borat*), appeared on *Aqua Teen Hunger Force*

Achievement: Coined Internet shorthand LMFAOWIHABFAFIMRAAM-MYAMTTDMRFBNA, which means "Laughing my figurative ass off while I have a Boba Fett action figure in my real ass and my mom yells at me to turn down my Rush *Fly by Night* album."

Age: 37

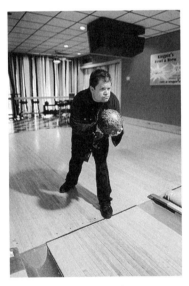

Bums: How many times have you seen *The Big Lebowski*?

Patton Oswalt: Way too many to count. The first time I saw it was on Friday, March 6, 1998, at a now-defunct theater in Sherman Oaks. And I saw it again at the New Beverly in Los Angeles, and afterwards we had a bowling party at the now-torn-down Hollywood Lanes, which is where I think they filmed it. That must've been around 2002. And then countless times on DVD.

Bums: A lot of people say that it took them a few viewings before they really got it. Was that the case with you? Upon which viewing of *The Big Lebowski* did you realize you were hooked?

PO: I can honestly say I was hooked on the first viewing. But I enjoyed myself too much to think of it as a "great" film, especially in the Coen brothers canon. That spot was reserved for *Fargo*. But as the years go on, *Lebowski* holds sway over all.

Bums: Who's your favorite character, and why?

PO: The Dude. I know I'm supposed to be all cinephile-y and pick the Jesus or Walter, but the Dude is one of the great characters in modern cinema.

Bums: If you were a *Big Lebowski* character, which one would you be?

PO: I dunno. It might be cool to be the Stranger, just to get to see what it feels like to be omniscient. But Jackie Treehorn seems to be having a good time. As much as I love the Dude, I'd hate to go through some of the stuff he goes through.

Yeah, Jackie Treehorn.

Bums: Do you have a favorite scene? A favorite line?

PO: My favorite scene is where the Dude is in the back of the limousine, trying to explain the "latest shit" to Lebowski. It's flawless. And my favorite line would have to be, "Fair?! Who's the nihilist, you bunch of fucking crybabies?"

Bums: What other movies would you consider yourself a huge fan of?

PO: Way too many to list. Off the top of my head, here's five: *Blast of Silence*, *American Movie*, *The Life and Death of Colonel Blimp*, *The Taking of Pelham One Two Three*, and *Charley Varrick*. There's about three hundred others.

Bums: Why do you think *The Big Lebowski* has connected so strongly with so many people?

PO: Because there's more than twice a week when we feel like the Dude, trying to unravel an already unraveling mystery, with our own chemical past getting in the way.

Bums: What is the most Dude thing you've ever done?

PO: Shopped in a bathrobe.

Also, did you take note of the fact that the three musicians who make cameos in the movie suffer increasing incidents of abuse? Jimmie Dale Gilmore is threatened with a gun, Flea gets hit in the nuts with a bowling ball, and Aimee Mann loses a toe.

Also, check out the almanac in the back of *The League of Extraordinary Gentlemen, Volume II*—one of the Dude's ancestors is mentioned.

Bums: The movie's plot is pretty complicated—if you had to sum up the movie in three sentences or less, how would you do it?

PO: Bowling noir.

Bums: As a writer yourself, how do you view the Coen brothers' writing?

PO: Sometimes it can be a little precious, but it's always fascinating.

Bums: Has what you love about the movie changed over time?

PO: Well, every time I watch it I notice something new and great, so, yeah.

Bums: If you could ask the Coen brothers one question about *The Big Lebowski*, what would it be?

PO: What's Jesus's day job?

Bums: What's your highest bowling score?

PO: It's pretty low. I suck at bowling.

Bums: What day is this?

PO: Uh, a weekday, isn't it?

Bums: Is it?

OLIVER BENJAMIN—Chiang Mai, Thailand

Name: Oliver Benjamin

Residence: Chiang Mai, Thailand/Los Angeles

Are you employed? Freelance journalist/graphic designer/unprofessional musician

Achievement: Founded Dudeism, "The world's slowest-growing religion."

Age: 38

Bums: Upon which viewing of *The Big Lebowski* did you realize you were hooked?

Oliver Benjamin: I first heard about *The Big Lebowski* from an English guy on a boat trip in Laos in 1998. He couldn't stop talking about it, using lines like "not the preferred nomenclature" and "shut the fuck up, Donny" over and over again. I'd never seen someone use lines from a movie in normal conversation, especially apropos of nothing, so naturally I thought he was nuts. When I got back to the States, no one had heard about it. So reluctantly I rented it one day and watched it three times in a row. Immediately hooked. I'd

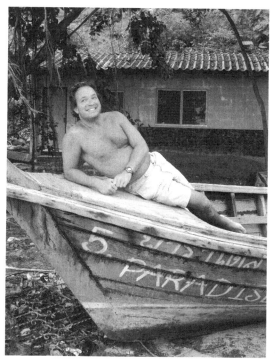

never seen anything like it. It's sad that the British got it right away and that it took folks in the U.S. so long. I think they respect complicated, over-the-top dialogue, whereas lots of Americans don't.

Bums: How has *The Big Lebowski* affected your life?

OB: Truth be told, I'm not naturally very Dudeish: I'm not so good at being unoccupied. The Dude's character reminds me that it's okay not to work so hard and try to do lots of stuff all the time. I think that very few people can really live the way the Dude does and still be happy, but that's why he's someone to inspire us, but not to totally emulate. If everyone were exactly like the Dude, the world would fall apart.

Bums: Who is your favorite character, and why?

OB: Of course the Dude, because there's never been any character like him before—an anti-hero not in the sense of being a bad guy, but in the sense of tossing aside the whole concept of heroism. Walter is trying to be a hero and, like many people who really try hard to be a hero, he's actually an asshole.

Bums: If you were a *Big Lebowski* character, which one would you be?

OB: I'd probably be a male version of Maude. I hang out with lots of weirdos here in Thailand and enjoy a leisurely, artistic life. My art has been commended as strongly marginal. I also love her dominating mastery of language. And, like her, I also find coitus a natural, zesty enterprise. Where we differ is that I have no problem with porn, no matter how ludicrous the story lines may be.

Bums: What is the most extreme length you've gone to express your love of *The Big Lebowski*?

> **Walter is trying to be a hero and, like many people who really try hard to be a hero, he's actually an asshole.**

OB: Starting a religion based around it.

Bums: What is your favorite scene?

OB: The initial scene where the Dude and Walter are screaming at each other, trying to have the most basic of conversations but incapable of communicating anything at all or listening to what the other is saying. It's the perfect representation of most modern relationships, either personal or political. Then, when Walter stops screaming for a second to gently admonish the agitated Dude for using an unintentionally racist term, it's as if the entire idiocy of modern morality is illuminated. Everybody thinks they know what's right and want to force it down your throat. But not the Dude. He sees the gray areas.

Bums: What other movies would you consider yourself a huge fan of?

OB: I prefer dialogue over plot any day. They say there are only like twelve plots anyway, so there can't be anything new, but a movie with good dialogue can blow your mind, and you can watch it over and over again. Today people quote movies like they used to quote literature and the Bible—it becomes part of who you are. So for me, the best movies are silly but deep comedies with unique, insightful dialogue, like *Office Space*, *Bull Durham*, *When Harry Met Sally*, *Grosse Pointe Blank*, and TV shows like *Arrested Development*.

Bums: When did you realize you weren't alone?

OB: One day in a small café in a small tourist town in Thailand, the movie was playing on TV and people from all over the world were crammed in together, howling with laughter. It was like being at a religious revival meeting.

Bums: How many times have you seen *The Big Lebowski*?

OB: About fifteen times. I try not to watch it too often, as I'm terrified one day I'll finally get sick of it.

Bums: Why do you think *The Big Lebowski* has such an effect on certain people like yourself?

OB: Because it's not like most other movies, in that it feels totally honest. Even though the characters and situations are totally outrageous, they all feel so familiar and authentic. Moreover, the issues the film brings up (war, heroism, power, individuality, freedom, morality, work) are more important now than ever before. And instead of bashing those issues over your head, it does so with a wink and a chuckle.

Bums: Who do you think Walter is talking to when he says, "Life does not stop and start at your convenience, you miserable piece of shit"?

OB: Some people think he's talking to Donny. But that's clearly impossible. Walter may have no patience for Donny, but he does not think he's a miserable piece of shit, and in fact loves him. Clearly he's referring to the wealthy Jeffrey Lebowski. Walter's just worried that the job Lebowski has given the Dude might interfere with their bowling schedule.

Bums: What is the most Dude thing you've ever done?

OB: I always forget what day it is, or if it's even a weekday. As a freelance writer who lives in a country where people work and go out drinking seven days a week, I hardly ever know what day it is. Or even what month.

Bums: Please give your own brief synopsis of *The Big Lebowski* in one breath.

OB: After being unfairly vandalized, a lazy man is convinced to stop being so passive and to set things straight, but then he's coerced into setting other things straight, and more things, until in the end he finds out that down deep, the world is fundamentally crooked, and it's probably better just to say "Fuck it" and go bowling with friends.

Bums: What is your favorite line?

OB: "Well, there isn't a literal connection."

Bums: How do you cope with those people in your life who just don't get it?

OB: I figure that most people have to watch the film about three times before they start to connect with it. It's like coffee or cigarettes or fine wine or stinky cheese.

Bums: Has what you love about the movie changed over time?

OB: The more I watch it, the more I see in it, so my love has gotten deeper. I'm now in my post-honeymoon, pre-midlife crisis stage.

Bums: If you could ask the Coen brothers one question about *The Big Lebowski*, what would it be?

OB: No matter what I'd ask them, I think they're too sly and oblique to ever give a straight answer.

Bums: What's your highest bowling score?

OB: I suck at bowling. Mostly gutters. I'm dead in the water.

Bums: What day is this?

OB: A good day.

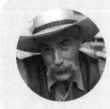

The Stranger Says . . .

"Fucking dog has fucking papers." The two prominent animals in the film are mislabeled. The "marmot" is a ferret and the "Pomeranian" is a terrier.

TONY HAWK—Carlsbad, California

Name: Tony Hawk

Residence: Carlsbad, California

Are you employed? Professional skateboarder, video game icon, the first to land a "900" (two and a half rotations before landing on the board)

Achievement: Staging the nail polish/pool scene with his wife as Bunny and friend passed out in the pool for *MTV Cribs*.

Age: 38

Bums: The word on the street is that you're a big fan of the movie. Is that true?

Tony Hawk: Oh, yeah. Very much.

Bums: Awesome. One of the stories we've heard is that when you guys are on tour, you'll occasionally knock off early and go to a bowling alley and drink some White Russians. Is that stuff true?

TH: We actually went to the bowling alley on tour once.

Bums: The Hollywood Star Lanes?

TH: Yeah, we made sure, because we were in L.A. on tour. We decided that we would do an outing and have it documented.

Bums: So did you pick up on *The Big Lebowski* pretty early on?

TH: Yeah, when I heard that the Coen brothers had a new movie out, I went and saw it right away. And then, once it came out on video, just watched it repetitively [*laughs*].

Bums: How many times do you think you've seen it?

TH: Well, let's put it this way: I have one movie that I've digitized for my iPod, my video iPod, and it's that movie.

Bums: So have you ever heard about the Lebowski Festival?

TH: Yeah, when it comes up each year, people always forward me the information. My friends find out about it, and . . . I think that's a little too much for me. I don't want to *role-play*. I just want to enjoy it.

At my house, when *MTV Cribs* came here, we set up this whole scene. They didn't use it—I was so bummed. My friend was in the pool, passed out on a raft. And then my wife was painting her toes. And we did the whole scene for them as if it was impromptu. I mean, she didn't say, "I'll suck your cock for a thousand dollars," but . . . yeah, we made it short enough that we thought they would actually use it. But they didn't end up using it. So if you happen to catch my *Cribs*, there is a scene where I walk by my wife and you

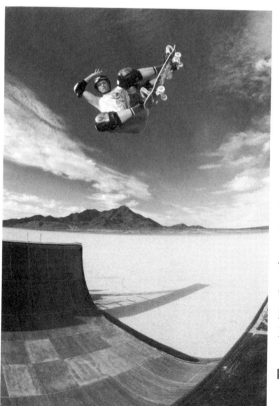

can see that she is doing something to her toes, and you can see my friend in the background passed out.

Bums: Well done, sir. Well done. It's funny, *The Big Lebowski* shows up all over the place in weird little pop-culture corners. There are some references in *The Power Puff Girls*, and there are fans everywhere. Do you know any other people who are into the movie?

TH: Shaun White is into it. He guest-deejayed on this radio station, and he played "What Condition My Condition Is In."

Bums: Do you have a favorite character?

TH: Donny.

Bums: Donny? Why Donny?

TH: Because somehow he's in, but he's so clueless. But he's still part of the crew—they include him on everything. Even though he doesn't know what's going on. You know what I mean? There's something about him that you love just because he's such an outcast. And, to be honest, it's really sad that he dies.

Bums: Yeah, didn't like seeing Donny go. The Coen brothers like to kill Steve Buscemi, though.

TH: Oh, yeah, I didn't think about that.

Bums: So what do you think it is about the movie that resonates with so many people? Why are people so into it?

TH: I think mainly the originality of the characters. And the extremes at which they are: the slacker Dude, and then there's the freaky artist, and the pseudo-aristocrat Lebowski. They're just all so over the top. But they work together. And then the German dudes— that's a whole ending unto itself.

I got married in January, and my friend, for a wedding gift, got an original print of Jeff Bridges's photo of when they were taking the Autobahn cover shoot. So he gave this original print, signed by Jeff Bridges, to us.

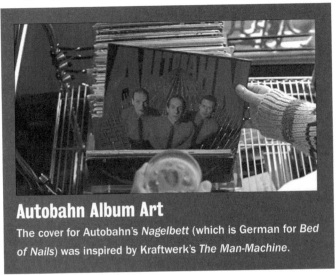

Autobahn Album Art
The cover for Autobahn's *Nagelbett* (which is German for *Bed of Nails*) was inspired by Kraftwerk's *The Man-Machine*.

Bums: What about a favorite scene?

TH: That's tough. I think one of my favorite scenes, even though it's short-lived, is when the Dude crashes.

Bums: When he runs into the dumpster?

TH: Yeah. It's so ridiculous that his roach gets caught under the seat, and he's freaking out, drinking a beer.

And then the homework. That's a lot to go through just to find the homework.

Bums: Do you ever find yourself quoting lines from the film?

TH: Phone's ringin', Dude.

Bums: Is that the one you quote most often?

TH: That's the easiest one.

Bums: It seems like they change over time. At first it's "Mark it 8, Dude" and "Over the line!" But then it becomes the more subtle ones.

TH: I do it all the time: "Nothing is fucked here, Dude," and "That's fucking interesting man, that's fucking interesting" are probably the most common. Sometimes I have to censor them with "effing," though.

Bums: What do you think about the Dude as a hero? Do you see the character of the Dude as a hero?

TH: In some ways—just by chance, though. It's not like he necessarily makes the right decisions, but he just happens to weave into wrapping things up. By circumstance. I think, just by the fact that he's sort of indifferent—not indifferent, but ineffective—is what makes him fix it all.

Bums: Yeah, in a backwards sort of way.

TH: Yeah. You know, one of my favorite lines that I use a lot, and rarely people get it, is if someone hands me a drink or fixes me a drink and it's really strong, I always tell them, "You make a hell of a Caucasian, Jackie." Rarely do they ever pick it up.

Bums: But when they do, it's magic, right?

TH: It is, yeah.

Bums: There's some bonding that goes on there.

TH: Exactly.

Bums: When you went to the Hollywood Star Lanes before they tore it down, what was that like?

TH: They had a display of some of the artifacts from the movie. So that was cool to see. I think I was more excited to see the outside, with the stars, than actually being inside. Because inside, when you're really there, it's a different perspective on how you pictured it, you know, where the bar is and where the lanes are. Because all that stuff gets distorted with how they shoot it. But getting to see the stars outside, and the parking lot where everything went down, was exciting. I mean, that's where Donny died.

Bums: Does *The Big Lebowski* get played a lot on the tour bus?

TH: Yeah. It's always at the front. It's kind of a common denominator among the crew. But I gotta say, it's really fun just watching it on airplanes on my iPod, too, all alone.

CRAIG McCRACKEN—Los Angeles

Name: Craig McCracken

Residence: Los Angeles

Are you employed? Creator of *The Powerpuff Girls* and *Foster's Home for Imaginary Friends* which can be seen on the Cartoon Network.

Achievement: Inserted several Lebowski references in both television shows and *The Powerpuff Girls Movie.*

Age: 35

Bums: Did you like *The Big Lebowski* the first time you saw it? If not, how many times did it take?

Craig McCracken: Well, like all Coen brothers' films I loved the visuals, the writing, and

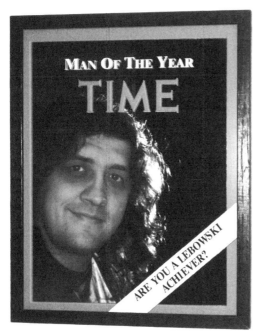

filmmaking right away, but as an overall film experience I was kinda confused. Walking out of the theater, I was like, "What just happened?" I knew I just saw something, but I wasn't quite sure what that something was. It wasn't until days later that it really began to sink into my psyche. Then after probably the second or third viewing, I realized it was one of the greatest movies I've ever seen.

Bums: How has *The Big Lebowski* affected your life?

CM: Every time I watch the film, it puts me in a really good mood. I just like the vibe of the whole thing. The Dude is a really inspirational character to me.

Bums: You have dropped some *Big Lebowski* references in your shows *The Powerpuff Girls* and *Foster's Home*. Well done, sir. Can you talk a little about your favorite references and what kind of response they have gotten?

CM: There was an episode of *Powerpuff Girls* where the Mayor's assistant, Ms. Bellum, was kidnapped and we aped the whole fireside ransom-note sequence. In another *Powerpuff Girls* episode, the Dude is seen on a bus. In the opening of *The Powerpuff Girls* movie, the shot of Professor walking through the grocery store is taken directly from the intro scene of the Dude. In *Foster's* we did a bowling episode called "The Big Lablooski" that featured a shot of Walter, Donny, and the Dude. The responses are pretty much a thumbs-up from those who pick up on the references. That, and getting to be interviewed for this book.

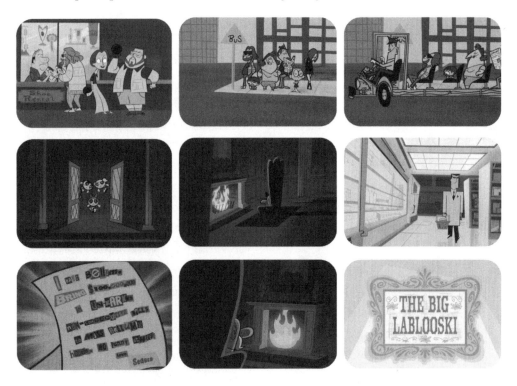

Bums: If you were a *Big Lebowski* character, which one would you be? Who is your favorite?

CM: Well, it's probably gonna be everyone's answer, but I really love the Dude and his whole perspective on life. He's like Buddha to me. Whether he knows it or not, he's achieved some sort of enlightenment. Like the Stranger says, "It's good knowing he's out there. The Dude, takin' 'er easy for all us sinners." I want to be like that someday.

Life Imitates Lebowski

Once you've watched the film a number of times, the world around you begins to change. When you see a bottle of Mr. Bubble you hear the songs of the humpback whale. Seeing a tumbleweed invokes the Stranger's voice in your head. Every time you see half and half in the grocery store you are tempted to sniff it for freshness instead of just checking the date. If there's a bowling pin, a ransom note, or a pair of dirty undies in a movie, you think, Is that a reference to *The Big Lebowski*? Some would say you're obsessed, and they'd probably be right.

No need to worry: You are not alone. Achievers are everywhere. They are writing for television shows, programming video games, opening restaurants, and forming bands. The following are a few of the places in the world we have seen *Lebowski* come to light.

The list below isn't meant to be comprehensive, but we do hope it gives you an idea of all the different areas in which Achievers work and play. New references are cropping up all the time. Check out the LebowskiFest.com forum or the "Big Lebowski in Popular Culture" article on Wikipedia.org for a more *thurrah* compilation.

On Television

• The 2006 season of *Veronica Mars* featured the following lines: "You're entering a world of pain, Larry!" and "Careful, man, there's a beverage here!"

• *Powerpuff Girls* creator Criag McCracken has succeeded in working in many lines of dialogue and caricatures of the Dude, Walter, and Donny into his cartoons. Many of the scenes he creates are homages to scenes from *The Big Lebowski*.

• In an episode of the CBS series *CSI: NY*, a man is accused of murdering his brother, whose body is found rolled up in a rug. The following dialogue is exchanged:
     Detective: "We found your brother in that fancy rug of yours."
     The accused: "He probably stole it on his way out."
     Detective: "What's he, a *Big Lebowski* fan? Just decided to take the rug for the heck of it?"

On the Internet(s)

• The website HomestarRunner.com features a character dressed as Walter Sobchak in a cartoon that takes place on Halloween.

- Several film shorts have been created with Lebowski dialogue dubbed over animation or video: *He-Man*, *Teenage Mutant Ninja Turtles*, *Monsters, Inc.*, *Brokeback Mountain*, and many others have been *Lebowskified*.

In Music

- Two bands that have performed at Lebowski Fests in New York and Seattle respectively, include the Prayers and Tears of Arthur Digby Sellers and the Fucking Eagles.

- A number of other bands have chosen lines of *Lebowski* dialogue for their names, including Give Us the Money, Lebowski, the Little Lebowski Urban Achievers, and Shut Up, Donny.

In Video Games

- In the 2002 *Spider-Man* video game, a training section called "Pinhead Bowling" features the voice of Bruce Campbell saying over the PA, "Jesus Quintana, your lane is ready, Jesus Quintana."

In Food

- Archie McPhee makes Nihilist Chewing Gum, which has absolutely no flavor.

- One of the "stunt rugs" used in filming the movie now hangs on the wall of La'Bowski's Restaurant in Lubbock, Texas.

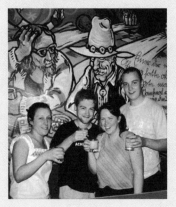

- Dresden, Germany, is home to a watering hole called the Lebowski-Bar. A giant, hand-painted mural features characters from the film, and they play the movie on a near-continuous loop.

- Oneida Lake, New York, is home to Lebowski's Sports Bar and Grill. One of their specialty subs is The Big Lebowski, a tasty concoction of steak, cheese, and garlic bread.

Bums: What is the most extreme length you've gone to express your love of *The Big Lebowski*?

CM: I was in a thrift store once and I came across the same sweater the Dude wears in the film. So I started wearing it every day, which led to this period where I sort of became the Dude. I already had the gut and the hair, so it wasn't long before I was shuffling around the studio in sloppy clothes and slippers and drinking White Russians at night. I stopped as soon as I met my wife. But the White Russian is still my drink of choice.

Bums: What is your favorite scene?

CM: It's really hard to pick a favorite, but I'll never forget the first time I saw the film. The last scene, where the Stranger breaks the fourth wall and delivers his monologue, totally blew me away. I couldn't believe how long it was going on, and the longer it went, the funnier it got. It's those types of scenes that make me love all the Coens' films. They push things so far it's almost cartoony. I've actually learned a lot about filmmaking and storytelling for cartoons from watching their films.

Bums: What other movie would you consider yourself a huge fan of?

CM: I typically like more obscure films. *The Adventures of Buckaroo Banzai Across the 8th Dimension*, *Mon Oncle*, and *Hitchhiker's Guide to the Galaxy* are on my desert-island list along with *The Big Lebowski*.

Bums: When did you realize you weren't alone?

CM: A few years after the film came out I would end up talking to people who were as into it as I was. My brothers-in-law and my cousin are fans. But I think it was when I first heard about the Lebowski Fest in '02 that I knew I wasn't the only one and there was something bigger going on.

Bums: How many times have you seen *The Big Lebowski*?

CM: Man, I don't know, probably around like fifteen, twenty times. It's the kind of film that

I'll just put on for a bit or watch when it happens to be on TV just to get a little fix. I watched it again to prepare for this interview so I could get in that space. Like I mentioned earlier, I like the whole vibe of the thing—it just makes me feel good. I enjoy it whole or in bits.

Bums: Why do you think *The Big Lebowski* has such an effect on certain people like yourself?

CM: Here's my theory: The protagonists in most movies are very proactive, they move the story forward, it's very wish-fulfillment storytelling. In *The Big Lebowski*, the Dude only actively moves the story forward twice. In the beginning he goes to the the Big Lebowski to get compensated for his rug, and in the end he goes back to the Big Lebowski to call him out. The rest of the film, the Dude is either being told to go somewhere or physically taken somewhere. He's being bounced around from one plot point to the next without his control, and he tries to do the best he can in each situation. This to me is much more like real life. Most people are not go-getter, A-type heroes. Most people try to do the best in whatever situation they happen to find themselves in, and they ultimately want to do the right thing and get back to doing what makes them happy.

> **I always saw the scene with the Stranger and the Dude as a sort of passing of the baton.**

Bums: What is the most Dude thing you've ever done?

CM: I didn't realize it at the time, but I was very Dude in college, if you know what I mean.

Bums: Please give your own brief synopsis of *The Big Lebowski* in one breath.

CM: Guy who's found his bliss loses it when he falls facedown in the muck. Does his best to get out of it and gets back to following his bliss.

Bums: What is your favorite line?

CM: "Careful, man, there's a beverage here!" Though in the TV dub of the film, the way they cleaned up "This is what happens when you fuck a stranger in the ass" is amazing. They translated it to "This is what happens when you find a stranger in the Alps." For some reason that line makes Walter seem even more like a nut.

Bums: How do you cope with those people in your life who just don't get it?

CM: Just smile, nod, and say, "Fuck it." It's like you said, some people just don't get it. It would be very un-Dude of me to force my views on them.

Bums: Has what you love about the movie changed over time?

CM: Not really changed, but definitely grown. I still love all the characters and the film's total vibe. But lately, as a Southern Californian, I've really begun to appreciate the portrayal of the city. It's not the typical Beverly Hills or East L.A. SoCal, but it's North Hollywood, Downtown, Venice, Pasadena, and as the opening scene acknowledges, it's still a desert and a part of the Old West.

Bums: If you could ask the Coen brothers one question about *The Big Lebowski*, what would it be?

CM: I always saw the scene with the Stranger and the Dude as a sort of passing of the baton. Here's what I mean: The Stranger is a cowboy, the quintessential symbol of America. In that scene it's almost as if he's telling the Dude that now he's the quintessential symbol of America. Like he says in the beginning, "He's the man for his time and place, he fits right in there." I'd like to ask them if I'm crazy.

Bums: What's your highest bowling score?

CM: I have no idea; I'm so bad I don't even bother keeping score.

Bums: What day is this?

CM: Sunday, November 5, 2006. I'm not Jewish, but in respect for Shomer Shabbos, I made sure not to do this interview on Saturday.

JOHNNY HICKMAN—Fort Collins, Colorado

Name: Johnny Hickman

Residence: Fort Collins, Colorado

Are you employed? Singer/songwriter/lead guitarist for Cracker

Achievement: Cofounded the band Cracker with David Lowery.

Age: 50

Bums: Upon which viewing of *The Big Lebowski* did you realize you were hooked?

Johnny Hickman: I believe the third or fourth. I was on our tour bus and watched it every night of that tour after the Cracker shows as we drove to the next town. By the fourth or fifth night I was making Caucasians for anyone who would watch with me.

Bums: How has *The Big Lebowski* affected your life?

JH: Not a day goes by that I don't quote a line of dialogue from *The Big Lebowski*. It's great

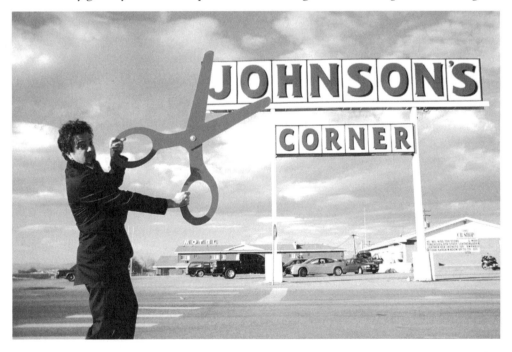

sport amongst we Achievers to find new and inventive ways to drop lines from *The Big Lebowski* into everyday situations to amuse ourselves and one another. Several of my friends and I were doing this almost from the first time we watched the film, and were delighted when we realized that it is common practice with any group of true Achievers.

Bums: Who is your favorite character, and why?

JH: It's a close tie with the Dude, but I have to go with Walter. He's a loose cannon and an insufferable know-it-all, yet he has a big, sensitive heart and really means well. And he is often right, isn't he? He is sentimental to a fault, which is also kind of endearing. Walter's got his friends' backs and they know it. He is as complex and aggro as the Dude is simple and laid-back, which makes their dynamic as a pair so wonderful. If I were in trouble I would want Walter by my side.

Bums: If you were a *Big Lebowski* character, which one would you be?

JH: I'm a slightly lazy man with an occasionally explosive temper, so perhaps that makes me sort of a cross between the Dude and Walter.

Bums: What is the most extreme length you've gone to express your love of *The Big Lebowski*?

JH: My wife deserves that honor for throwing me a *Big Lebowski* party for my fiftieth birthday. It was held in a bowling alley complete with constantly flowing Caucasians, a case of Sioux City sarsaparilla, and even a rug-pissers cake that she helped design. She had a widescreen brought in for viewing *The Big Lebowski*. My favorite moment was having my teenaged nephews and bandmates quote the dialogue right with me. I was so proud it brought me to tears. I also have a framed *Big Lebowski* movie poster that my nineteen-year-old son bought me a few years ago. It hangs in a place of honor right by my gold records and . . . what have you.

Bums: What is your favorite scene?

JH: The Dude's first meeting with the millionaire Lebowski. The dialogue, the polarity between the two characters, the gestures, the body language, the way it's shot, is pure genius.

Bums: What other movies would you consider yourself a huge fan of?

JH: My other favorite movie is *The Elephant Man*, directed by David Lynch. It's as opposite as you could get from *The Big Lebowski* in terms of mood. I watch *The Big Lebowski* to laugh and *The Elephant Man* to cry. I consider them both nearly perfect films. They are the only two films I own that I constantly implore others to watch with me. First runner-up would be *Fargo*.

Bums: When did you realize you weren't alone?

JH: When I remember a former roadie of Cracker named Jeff Mayes watching *The Big Lebowski* over and over in the back lounge of the tour bus. Jeff soon moved into a California bungalow and then realized it was in the complex the Dude lived in! Curvy sidewalk and all! After the tour I found his copy of the film and began my own addiction. My finest moment of *The Big Lebowski* camaraderie came when my band played in Louisville, Kentucky, and you guys introduced yourselves to me. We had dinner together, and you allowed me a peek into your madness at the office later. It was a day that changed my life forever.

Bums: How many times have you seen *The Big Lebowski*?

JH: At least one hundred, probably more. I own two copies of the DVD so that I am never far from it at home or on tour.

Bums: Why do you think *The Big Lebowski* has such an effect on certain people like yourself?

JH: I consider it the definitive buddy movie for our times. It really has it all. A great story line, brilliantly conceived characters, mystery, thrills, high drama, and, above and beyond all else, it's one of the funniest movies ever made, in my opinion.

Bums: What is the most Dude thing you've ever done?

> ## Some viewers will simply enjoy it as that and move on with their lives. For others it becomes a way of life.

JH: My post-tour ritual is very Dude. When I get off the road the very first thing I do is put on my robe. Then I wander around the house sipping Caucasians, listening to and largely ignoring phone messages. I also light candles and listen to brainless New Agey music in the tub. Of course no one has ever tossed a ferret, or "marmot," in there with me. Aside from the Caucasians, I've done these things for years, even pre–*The Big Lebowski*. The Dude taught me the wonder of White Russians as medication from everyday stress.

Bums: Please give your own brief synopsis of *The Big Lebowski* in one breath.

JH: This film is a side-achingly funny tale of mistaken identity and the subsequent chain of events that occurs. Some viewers will simply enjoy it as that and move on with their lives. For others it becomes a way of life. I am one of those, and I make no apologies for it.

Bums: What's your favorite line?

JH: "Yes! Fuck it! That's your answer. That's your answer for everything! Tattoo it on your forehead!"

Bums: How do you cope with those people in your life who just don't get it?

JH: I don't have many close friends who don't get it. If someone does not get *The Big Lebowski* then they probably don't have much of a sense of humor, and life is too short to spend it around those people.

Bums: Has what you love about the movie changed over time?

JH: Yes. That's part of the beauty of being an Achiever. You find new things to love. Of course, nothing beats those first few moments when I take my first sip of Caucasian and hear the first notes of "Tumbling Tumbleweeds." At that moment, all is right in the world.

Bums: If you could ask the Coen brothers one question about *The Big Lebowski* what would it be?

JH: Gentlemen, will you please consider coming to one of the Lebowski Fests for a question-and-answer session? Don't be afraid, we are harmless. Like Trekkies, only slightly hipper and more relaxed.

Bums: What's your highest bowling score?

JH: 149. I'm no Donny.

Bums: What day is this?

JH: I have not checked my calendar, so I have no frame of reference.

ALYSHA NAPLES—San Francisco

Name: Alysha Naples

Residence: San Francisco

Are you employed? Graphic designer/university professor

Achievement: Trivia champion at the Fifth Annual Lebowski Fest in 2006.

Age: 31

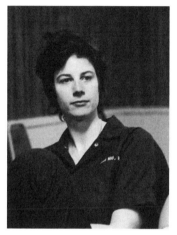

Bums: Looking back: How would you say that *The Big Lebowski* has affected your life?

Alysha Naples: Well, it's definitely changed my vocabulary.

Bums: For better or for worse?

AN: I don't know. Not necessarily for better, but I definitely find that I tend to use a lot of *Lebowski* phrases, especially in the classroom, and it's always really interesting to me to see which of my students laugh and which don't. And then, of course, they start misquoting it at me, and then I have to cringe.

Bums: Do you think there are any characteristics that distinguish the *Lebowski* fans from your other friends?

AN: I think that we drink more than they do. All of my friends, part of the community or not, are at least people who enjoy the movie. Nobody takes it quite to the level that I do within my friends that I haven't met through the Lebowski Fest forum. I would just say on the whole that Achievers are a bit of a drunker group.

Bums: Who is your favorite character and why?

AN: This is tough. I hated Walter the first time I saw it, but now I think he's totally genius. Although he's such an asshole that I don't think I could say that he's my favorite. And then

> ## And there is something about knowing that everyone isn't going to get this joke that I think makes us appreciate it all the more.

the Dude, of course, but I don't really relate, because I think I'm probably the only Achiever who doesn't smoke pot.

But for some reason, as great as the main characters are, I think the real genius of the movie is in the supporting cast. Is it Jesus, Brandt, the Stranger, Jackie Treehorn, her costar in the beaver picture? I don't know. Brandt, Philip Seymour Hoffman, is so brilliant, and his performance is so nuanced, that even though I've seen it maybe about a hundred times, Brandt still gets me. Every time.

Bums: What's the most extreme length you've gone to to express your love for *The Big Lebowski?*

AN: Well, I would say that three thousand miles that I have gone each way to Louisville to the Lebowski Fest. Three times. With flash cards. And custom-made bowling coveralls. I've knitted probably thirty wristbands for forum Achievers. And in my basement I have a bench from the Hollywood Star Lanes.

Bums: What about a favorite scene from the movie?

AN: Um, I'd have to think the opening bowling scene, where the Dude is talking about his rug. It really ties the movie together. There is something about that scene that—while there are others that I think are equally well put together—there is something about that scene and how it really establishes so much about the characters and the relationships between them, while having a completely nonsensical discussion in so many ways, that I think is just fantastic.

Bums: What is it about the movie that has such a huge effect on certain people like yourself?

AN: It's smart and funny. But I think the smart part is the really important part. It's subtle. There is something in the humor that I think to some extent we're kind of like the same people that like the bands that nobody else has heard of.

And there is something about knowing that everyone isn't going to get this joke that I think makes us appreciate it all the more. There's something about working for the laugh that I think we appreciate.

Bums: Final question: What day is this?

AN: Is it already the tenth?

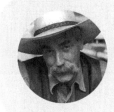

The Stranger Says . . .
"Dude!" The word *dude* and its variations (*Duder*, *His Dudeness*, et cetera) are said 160 times.

The Academic Symposium—
Louisville, Kentucky

In conjunction with the 2006 Lebowski Fest in Louisville, Kentucky, two professors/ friends/Coen brothers fanatics were inspired to hold an academic symposium focusing on *The Big Lebowski.* Edward Comentale, an associate professor of English at Indiana University, and Aaron Jaffe, an assistant professor of English at the University of Louisville, put out a call for papers to their academic brethren with the aim of "inventing a critical program equal to the tasks of interpreting *The Big Lebowski* and addressing the fan cult that has quickly grown in its wake."

In response, they received more than eighty submissions from cultural commentators, critics, theorists, and scholars of all stripes. Among the two dozen papers selected were "Dudespeak," "Figurin' the Fuckin' Carpet," and "I Hate the Eagles: *The Big Lebowski* Meditates on Musical Genre." (A full list of papers is included at the end of this section.)

When Comentale and Jaffe put out their call for papers, they included the following "Letter to Donny" by way of explanation. With their permission, we've included it here. They'd love it if you would read it and give them notes.

To: Donald Kerabatsos
From: Edward Comentale and Aaron Jaffe
Re: A Frame of Reference
Date: September 11, 2006

Sorry we missed you at our meeting with the creators of Lebowski Fest at Lynn's Paradise Cafe in Louisville, Kentucky.

The order of the day was how to bring brainpower to their annual celebration of all things Lebowski.

On the one hand, amidst all the White Russians, sarsaparillas, and bowling, Lebowski fans, aka "Achievers," love nothing better than to spout all manner of high-falutin' theory about the movie we all admire.

On the other hand, we like to spout high-falutin' theory all the time, but all too rarely get to do it while we drink oat sodas and bowl.

A symbiosis was born.

The symposium.

In a bowling alley, we said.

Like, what's a symposium, they said?

Don't worry about it, we said.

And yet we worried anyway, as is our nature . . .

The Coen brothers have drawn together an unusual cult. Walking the line between brainy French philosophy and Tinseltown schmaltz, they taunt and tantalize a legion of overeducated and underemployed slackers. Heidegger *avec* Hula Hoop. Ulysses in hair pomade. Saddam Hussein in bowling shoes. The Big Lebowski, the Big Other—sprinkle in loads of ins 'n' outs to confuse the theory and the amusement. Each movie, a cosmic thingamajig, urging us westward ho, spinning the best and worst of twentieth-century Americana into its great, glorious pinwheel!

Somewhere in this, a new kind of fan culture is born: dark post-postmodern dopamine—part mental, part visceral, always dark, and always hysterical. Fans too smart, too dumb, too lazy, too snobby, too T-shirted, too sullen, too partial to road food for their own good—known to pontificate wildly about Heisenberg and then micturate (Is *that* even a word? Yes, it is.) on the Technicolor carpets. For us, the "Achievers," any difference between fans and scholars is strictly academic.

No degree required, but can't it all be a little enhanced with some knowledge of film history, literary theory, Southern radio, nihilism, and Jewish mysticism? You should have to watch Coen stuff to earn your degree, we thought. And to prove it, we've taught college classes on the Coens to teach our students that, paraphrasing Socrates now, sometimes stupid is just another name for smart. How can something so pretentious be so puerile? One "Achiever" put it best: "Thinking about Coen movies is impossible—you'd have to think of something that they're not already thinking, and they're thinking about everything."

For the "over-Achiever," then, the question is not what we can do for *The Big Lebowski*, but what *The Big Lebowski* can do for us. How can Coen-style genre-scrambling, style-swaggering, kinetotheorizing, mouth-breathing stupidity help us invent a new way of doing a scholarly conference, fostering quick 'n' dirty intellectual exchange and community accompanied by cracking kingpins? Can we bring fans and academics (who are, after all, fans of fans) back together again?

The symposium bull pen included a shocking range of perspectives from "Achievers" across the U.S. and Canada, both inside and out of the university, joining together to discuss potential frames of reference for a movie and all its cultural baggage. Some thirty professors and movie critics—academic and nonacademic layabouts of all stripes—hunkered down to talk Lebowski in a bowling alley meeting room for two days before Lebowski Fest '06.

With the Dude's addled attention span as our guide, the program departed from the usual format of academic conferences: papers were shorter, approaches more varied, leaving lots more time for the greasy lane food and wild-eyed discussion we love. Panelists spoke on a host of topics related to the movie (interior design, silent film, industrial chemicals, Brunswick, Raymond Chandler, Rip Van Winkle, etc.) and show off a ridiculous range of approaches (linguistics, history, psychoanalysis, rhetorical analysis, cultural studies, media studies, informatics, library science, anthropology, etc.). One professor just talked about why he looked like the Dude.

In the end, we all remembered to take comfort in the Dude's immortal words: "Hey, man, why don't you fucking listen occasionally? You might learn something."

We remain, like you, Donny, children who wander into the middle of a movie. Abidingly . . .

IS THIS YOUR HOMEWORK, LARRY? SYMPOSIUM PAPERS

• Dennis Allen, West Virginia University: "Logjammin' and Gutterballs: Masculinities in *The Big Lebowski*"

• Fred Ashe, Birmingham-Southern College: "Love and Death and the Dude Van Winkle"

• Matthew Biberman, University of Louisville: "Lebowski *avec* Lacan: Rethinking Freud's Comic Logic"

• Tom Byers, University of Louisville: "He's the Man for His Time . . . : Lebowski Generations"

• Bradley Clissold, Memorial University, St. Johns, Canada: "Fuck It, Dude, Let's Go Bowling: The Antecedent Cultural Connotations of Bowling in *The Big Lebowski*"

• Ed Comentale, Indiana University: "Where the Pavement Ends and the West Begins: Some Notes on Frontiers and Gestures in *The Big Lebowski*"

• Todd Comer, Defiance College: "You're Like a Child Who Wanders into the Middle of a Movie: Birth and Representational Violence in *Fargo* and *The Big Lebowski*"

• Alan Dale, Independent Scholar: "The Coen Brothers: A World of Irony"

• Steve Davis, Indiana University: "The Noir That Wasn't There: *The Big Lebowski*, Film Noir, and Postmodern Cinema"

• Emily Dill and Karen Janke, Indiana University/Purdue University at Indianapolis: "New Shit Has Come to Light: The Information-Seeking Behavior of the Dude"

• Jonathan Elmer, Indiana University: "Abiding and Enduring"

• Richard Gaughran, James Madison University: "Professor Dude: An Inquiry into the Appeal of His Dudeness for Contemporary College Students"

• Thomas Giannotti, California State University, Dominguez Hills: "Lebowski/Mnemosyne: Cultural Memory, Cultural Authority, and Forgetfulness"

• Dennis Hall, University of Louisville: "Figurin' the Fuckin' Carpet"

• Aaron Jaffe, University of Louisville: "Brunswick/Fluxus"

• Josh Kates, Indiana University: "What's the Difference? The Dude or Paul de Man as True Heir to the Sixties"

• Justus Nieland, Michigan State University: "Dudespeak"

• Marc Ouellette, McMaster University: "Don't Fuck with the Jesus: *The Big Lebowski*, Ritual and (Imposed) Narratives of the Self"

• Diane Pecknold, University of Louisville: "I Hate the Eagles: *The Big Lebowski* Meditates on Musical Genre"

• Chris Raczkowski, University of South Alabama: "The Competing Noir Daddies of the Coen Brothers"

• Andrew Rabin, University of Louisville: "Well, It's Not a Literal Connection, Dude: History, Allegory and the Medieval Grail Quest in *The Big Lebowski*"

• William Preston Robertson, Writer and Filmmaker: "Chuckleheaded Beacon in an Existential Night: A Brief History of the Bowling Noir Film Genre with Some Post Modernist Neo-Noir Afterthoughts"

• Judith Roof, Michigan State University: "Size Matters"

• Stacy Thompson, University of Wisconsin, Eau Claire: "Obscene Enjoyment and the Port Huron Statement"

• Steve Wender, Independent Scholar: "What Condition the Postmodern Condition Is In: Collecting Culture in *The Big Lebowski*"

• Alisha Wheatley, Independent Scholar: "Lebowski Fest Through the Looking Glass: Electronic Media and Live Performance"

CHAPTER SIX

LEBOWSKI FEST.
IF YOU WILL IT, DUDE, IT IS NO DREAM

Lebowski Fest? What in God's holy name are you blathering about?

In case your boss has ever asked you to explain what exactly a Lebowski Fest is, or if you're a concerned parent worried that your child has joined a cult of bathrobe-wearing, White-Russian-swilling nihilists, here's the gist.

Lebowski Fest is a festival that celebrates the Coen brothers' 1998 cult comedy, *The Big Lebowski*. A typical Lebowski Fest spans two days. The first day centers around live music followed by a midnight screening of *The Big Lebowski*. Hundreds and sometimes thousands of fans, aka Achievers, watch the movie, drink White Russians, shout out lines of dialogue, dress in costume, and perhaps partake in a little what have you. The event's second day takes place at a bowling alley, and Achievers often dress up as their favorite characters or even as lines of dialogue. We've seen everything from fans dressed as the queen in her damned undies to the pope shitting in the woods to a Vietnam soldier who died facedown in the muck. Once they've secured a lane, fans run amok in the bowling alley, spurred on by Creedence and other great tunes. They enjoy (much) more drinking of White Russians and participate in trivia, farthest-traveled, highest-bowler, and costume contests. The third day is never discussed, as it usually involves waking up with a severed toe in your pocket and a marmot curled up next to you. The shame can be unbearable.

You may think we're joking, and perhaps you're right. When we started Lebowski Fest in 2002, it was a joke of sorts. We just had no idea there would turn out to be so many other fans out there who would think it's funny. With each year, it keeps getting bigger and weirder and more ridiculous. The Achievers keep showing up to sold-out events in Louisville, New York, Los Angeles, Las Vegas, Austin, Seattle, and the UK!

Please to enjoy this somewhat chronological catalogue, *Adventures in Lebowski Fest.*

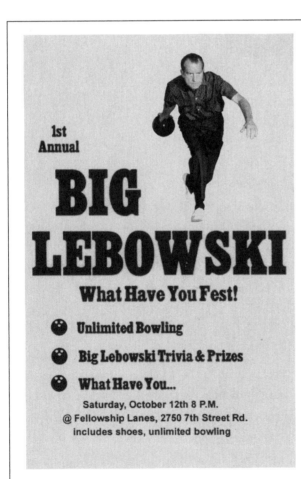

First Annual Big Lebowski What-Have-You Fest

The First Lebowski Fest (or First Annual Big Lebowski What-Have-You Fest, if you're not into the—well, you know . . .) was held in October 2002 at the Fellowship Lanes in Louisville, Kentucky. The Fellowship Lanes are located smack in the heart of Louisville's 7th Street Road, which is easily the city's seediest thoroughfare. (Anyone who asked a local for directions that night might have gotten a response like, "Turn left at the Foxy Lady, then go straight past the White Collar Stag Bar & Lounge . . . if you pass the Classie Lady, you've gone too far.")

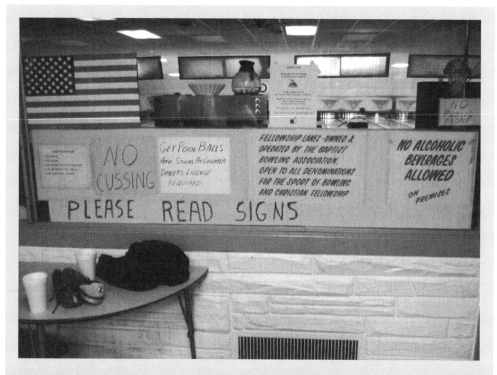

PLEASE READ SIGNS

Considering the surroundings, the NO LAP DANCES sign was conspicuously absent.

And yet strangely enough, the first thing to greet Achievers as they entered the bowling alley was a set of large signs full of prohibitions like NO CUSSING and NO ALCOHOLIC BEVERAGES ALLOWED. Below these signs was another sign directing the reader to read the signs above it. The Fellowship Lanes' high-minded temperance was soon explained by yet another sign: ALL DENOMINATIONS WELCOME FOR THE SPORT OF BOWLING AND CHRISTIAN FELLOWSHIP. Were they serious? Yes, they were, and they didn't care that the Supreme Court has roundly rejected prior restraint. Our plans to screen the movie during the evening went out the window when our host asked, "Is there cussin' in that?" Lesson learned: Do your homework before you pick your venue!

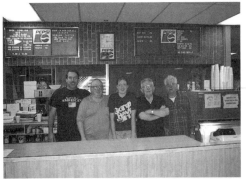

That's the look of some satisfied Baptists. By the end of the night they'd sold their entire stock of 120 hot dogs.

Despite all that—or maybe in part because of it—the Lanes lived up to their name and there was a feeling of true fellowship in the air. The costume contest was won by a fifteen-year-old Jesus Quintana from Indianapolis who sported a glued-on goatee and a set of purple scrubs that had been custom-embroidered by his mom. The Farthest Traveled award went to two fellas who flew in from Tucson. And—inspired by a group of high school kids from Buffalo, who skipped school the day before on the pretext of "visiting colleges," drove into the middle of the night, slept in their car while parked in a dairy field, got towed while at breakfast, and still made it to the Fest on time—we created a Hardest Traveled prize on the spot and have continued to award it at every Lebowski Fest since.

Nick Peskoe, costume contest winner. It don't matter to Jesus.

Although we'd been expecting only twenty or so of our friends to come out, more than 150 people showed up to bowl a few frames, have a few laughs, and drink a few—er, Diet Pepsis.

Looking back, it's hard to imagine the Lebowski Fest having a more perfect beginning.

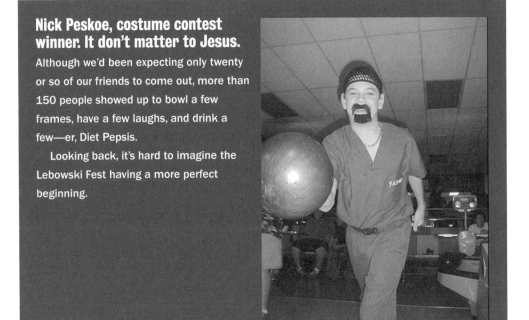

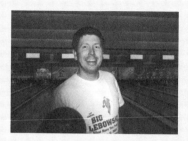

Our first celebrity:

Mike Walsh of BowlingRoadtrip.com, who was in the middle of fulfilling his ambition to bowl in all fifty states, scrapped plans to bowl with funeral directors in Philly to be on hand that night.

Second Annual Lebowski Fest

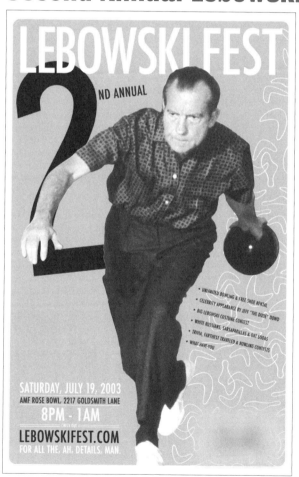

LEBOWSKI FEST

2ND ANNUAL

- UNLIMITED BOWLING & FREE SHOE RENTAL
- CELEBRITY APPEARANCE BY JEFF "THE DUDE" DOWD
- BIG LEBOWSKI COSTUME CONTEST
- WHITE RUSSIANS, SARSAPARILLAS & OAT SODAS
- TRIVIA, FARTHEST TRAVELED & BOWLING CONTESTS
- WHAT HAVE-YOU

SATURDAY, JULY 19, 2003
AMF ROSE BOWL, 2217 GOLDSMITH LANE
8PM - 1AM
LEBOWSKIFEST.COM
FOR ALL THE, AH, DETAILS, MAN.

Floating for months on the high of the First Annual experience, we locked down the domain LebowskiFest.com, launched an official website (the word *official* meaning that it now contained more than one page), and started laying plans for a sequel. There would definitely be alcohol, a bigger bowling alley and better prizes, a screening of the film—and enough cursing to make the Stranger blush.

By chance an intern at *Spin* magazine found the website and, as a joke, submitted the Fest for inclusion in their list of "19 Events You Can't Afford to Miss This Summer." When the issue came out, there it was alongside Lollapalooza and Snoop Dogg: "Bowl with Jesus."

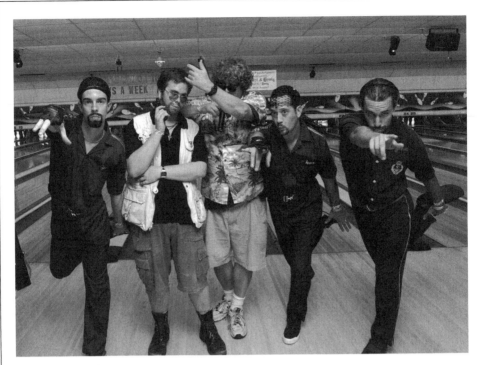

Dios Mio! Jeff Dowd attends his first Lebowski Fest.

That little blurb put the Lebowski Fest on the map, and when the Fest kicked off that June, more than twelve hundred Achievers attended from thirty-five states and parts of Canada. The Second Annual marked a lot of firsts for Lebowski Fest: first appearance by Jeff "The Dude" Dowd, first screening of the film, first appearance by the Lebowskimobile, and the inaugural Ringer Toss. (Yes, we put several pair of dirty undies in a bag and tossed them out the window of the Lebowskimobile.)

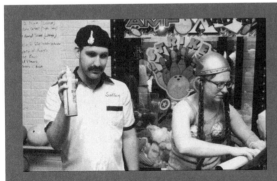

This aggression will not stand, man.

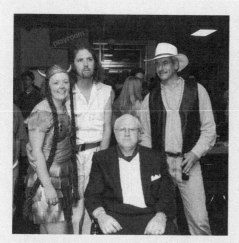

Did I urinate on your rug?

All in all, another magical evening. What it lost in intimacy from the First Annual, it gained in its feeling of holy shitness. This was the first time so many Achievers had gathered in one place, the first experience of collective Lebowski devotion/delusion.

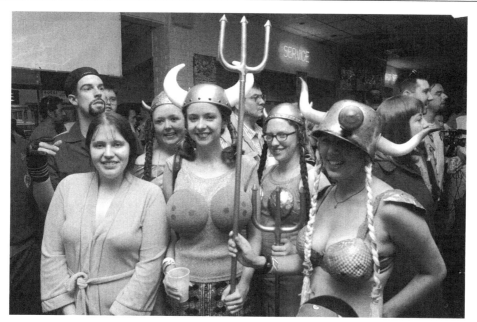

Just dropped in

And it was all capped at the end of the night by a perfect final moment. As the last guests were straggling away, the bowling alley's manager, Rodney, came out to lock up. He looked down to notice the Oriental rug that had been placed at his front door. He chased after the Lebowskimobile as it pulled into the darkness, waving his hands and screaming, "Wait! Come back! You forgot your rug!"

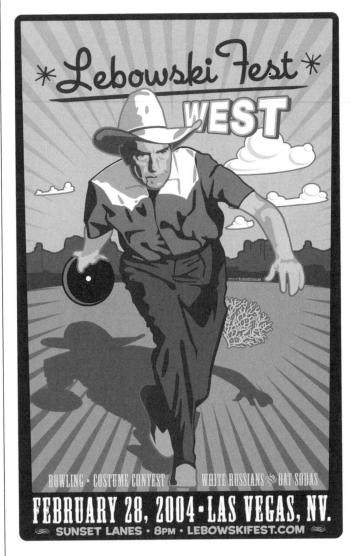

Lebowski Fest West, Las Vegas

High demand and a great poster by Bill Green pulled the Fest out West to Vegas in February 2004. This Fest marked the first appearance by an actor from the film. Jim Hoosier, who played Liam, the Jesus's bowling buddy, took the podium to introduce the film before the Friday-night screening. The reception he received was of rock-star proportions—the fuckin' Eagles should be so lucky. When he stepped out, produced his ball shammy, and did his patented ball-polishing maneuver and slow-mo belly jiggle, the crowd roared. No one was more surprised than Jim.

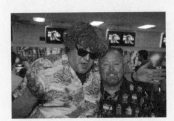

**Liam and me:
Jeff Dowd poses with Jim Hoosier.**

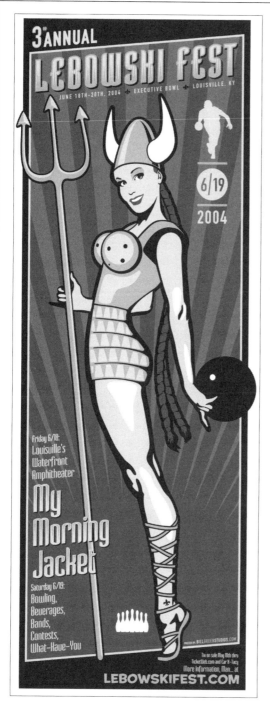

Third Annual Lebowski Fest

Seeing how the movie has a kick-ass soundtrack, it only seemed natural to add live music to the Fest. In summer 2004, we invited My Morning Jacket to headline the Third Annual Fest at Louisville's Waterfront Amphitheater. When they took the stage the entire band was dressed as characters from the film, including Jim James in the Dude's bathrobe. They opened with Dylan's "The Man in Me," and fireworks filled the sky.

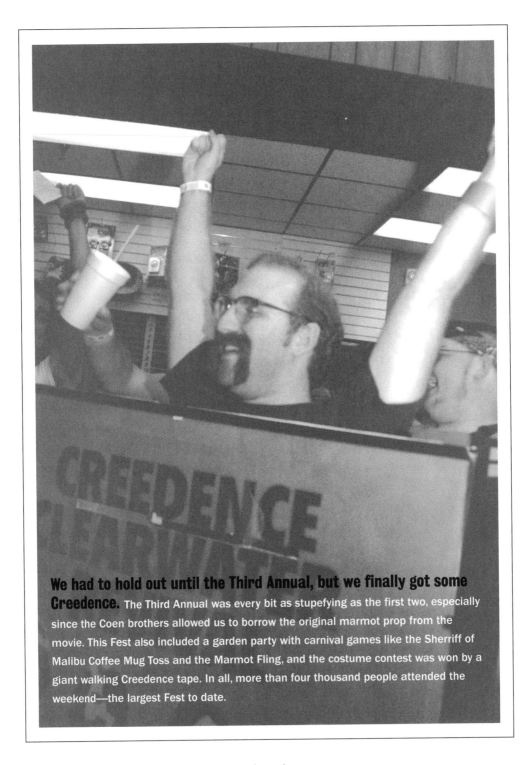

We had to hold out until the Third Annual, but we finally got some Creedence. The Third Annual was every bit as stupefying as the first two, especially since the Coen brothers allowed us to borrow the original marmot prop from the movie. This Fest also included a garden party with carnival games like the Sherriff of Malibu Coffee Mug Toss and the Marmot Fling, and the costume contest was won by a giant walking Creedence tape. In all, more than four thousand people attended the weekend—the largest Fest to date.

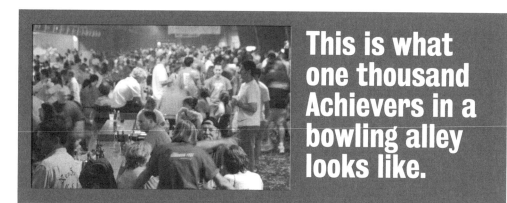

This is what one thousand Achievers in a bowling alley looks like.

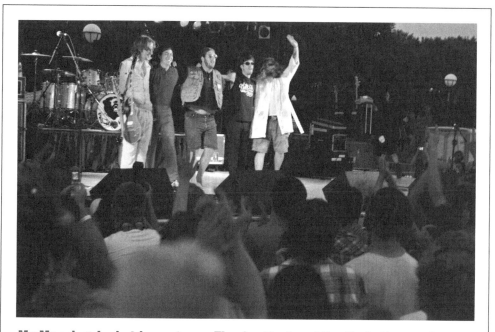

My Morning Jacket in costume: They're the band for their time and place.

Jeff Dowd once again dropped in to see what condition the Achievers were in. The morning after he arrived, while with us on the way to a local TV appearance, he decided to do some research on the host and learned that she was a former Chicago Bulls cheerleader. Live on the air, he turned to her at one point and said, "Remember that night in Chicago? It was me, you, and Dennis Rodman? You'd had a few drinks so you might not remember . . . " You can imagine where it went from there.

To add to the Dude's antics that morning, on the way home, in order to remember part of a story, he had to call MC Hammer on his cell phone. He had Hammer on speed dial.

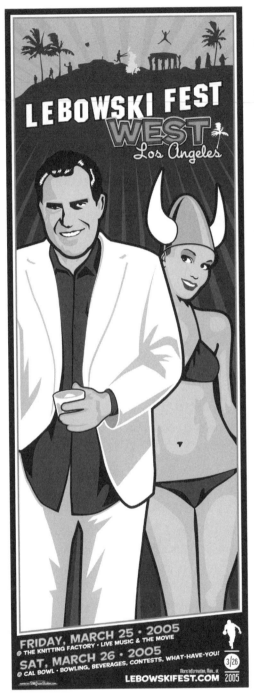

Lebowski Fest West, Los Angeles

They call Los Angeles the "city of angels," but we didn't find it to be that exactly. We did have a hell of a time, however, seeing as eight of the actors from the film came out to sign autographs, including David Huddleston (the Big Lebowski), Robin Jones (Ralphs Checkout Girl), Jack Kehler (Marty the Landlord), Peter Stormare (Uli the Nihilist), Jerry Haleva (Saddam), and Lu Elrod (the waitress from the diner where Walter enjoys his coffee).

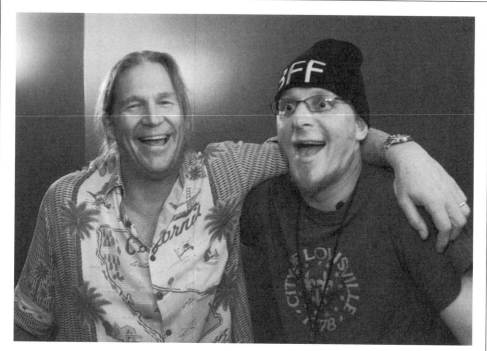

Topping it all, though, was the moment when we got to raise the curtain and say, "Ladies and gentlemen, Jeff Bridges!"

The Dude himself came out with his band to play a set of music from his new album and some covers from the film's soundtrack. Jeff Bridges is just as cool and Dudelike as you would hope him to be. He drinks a Russian (vodka on the rocks) instead of a White Russian, and he wore the same jelly sandals that he'd worn in the movie.

When one of us asked about his jellies, he responded, "What size do you wear?" As fate would have it, one of us was roughly a match. Jeff Bridges tossed one across the room and said, "Try it on, man. They're really comfortable." The lucky recipient slipped off his shoe, but Bridges stopped him just as he began to replace it with the sandal. "No, man, you gotta take your sock off," he said. "I want you to get the full experience."

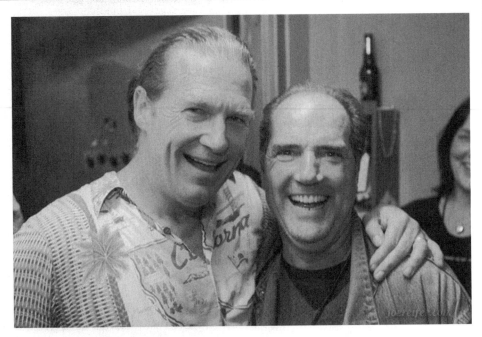

Ah, Dude, it's already the tenth: Jeff Bridges and Jack Kehler

Other highlights from that weekend were Peter Stormare and his band, Blonde from Fargo, and the first appearance of Autobahn live in concert. A couple traveled all the way from Ecuador to L.A. and got engaged in the bowling alley. There were also some unexpected celebrity guests who attended, including John Flansburgh from They Might Be Giants and actor Jeff Cohen, who played none other than Chunk in *The Goonies*! Even though he did not have a ticket to the sold-out event, we let him in without asking him to do the Truffle Shuffle.

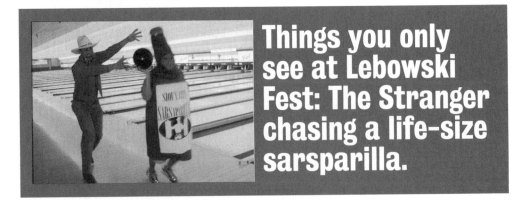

Things you only see at Lebowski Fest: The Stranger chasing a life-size sarsparilla.

Jeff "The Dude" Dowd and the mayor of Louisville, Jerry Abramson, just after presenting the Dude with the key to the city for his various civic, ah . . .

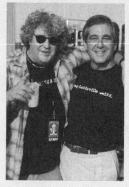

Later that year, the Fourth Annual Lebowski Fest featured They Might Be Giants as the musical headliner with Corn Mo—an unholy combination of Jack Black and Meat Loaf—as support. The Lebowski Lunch Radio Hour included some great covers from the soundtrack including "I Got It Bad (and That Ain't Good)," sung by Louisville's own Will Oldham. The mayor of Louisville presented Jeff Dowd with a key to the city. Ironically, the Dude would find himself without a ride back to the hotel that very night. The garden party was taken to the next level with a Lebowski-themed burlesque show. The costume contest was won by the Camel Fuckers.

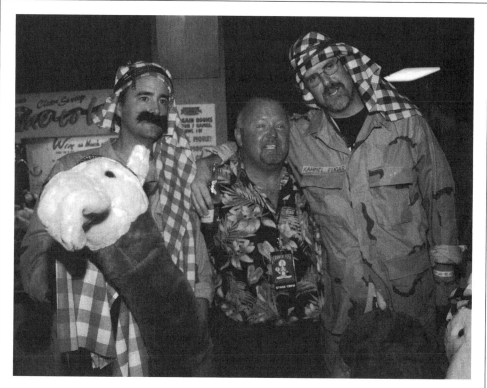

Liam (Jim Hoosier) and costume-contest winners the Camel Fuckers.

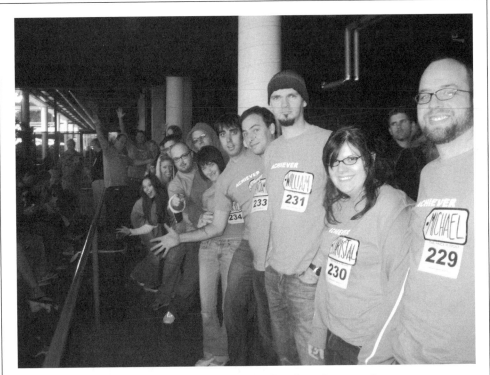

Achievers on line for *The Price Is Right.* During the preshow warmup, a stupefied Bob Barker looked at us and asked, "Well, what have you achieved?"

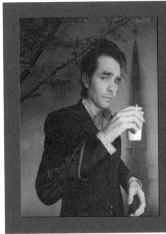

Next we landed in Austin, Texas, where we met "Big" Lew Abernathy, who was the private-detective friend of Peter Exline, who thought it was a good idea to put the homework in a baggie and go brace the kid. (See his interview page 106.)

The Fifth Annual Lebowski Fest in Louisville included our first double-feature screening of *Raising Arizona* and *The Big Lebowski.* It was the first time we held a Lebowski-themed art show as well as an academic symposium examining the "Cult of Lebowski." The musical guests were Jon Spencer's Heavy Trash and the Sadies. The Seattle Fest featured an amazing performance by Har Mar Superstar.

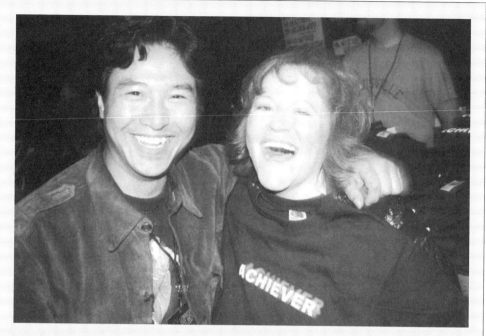

Among our special guests in L.A. were Jim Hoosier (Liam), Luis Colina (Corvette Owner), Peter Exline (one of the inspirations for the story), Jeff Dowd, and Edie McClurg of *Ferris Buehler's Day Off*! What does Edie have to do with *The Big Lebowski*? Who cares, it's Mrs. Poole! Edie performed in a zydeco band playing the frattoir (washboard, for the non-cajun), and knocked our socks off. These are just a few highlights from our adventures in Lebowski. The following pages are a collection of event posters designed by the lovable Bill Green.

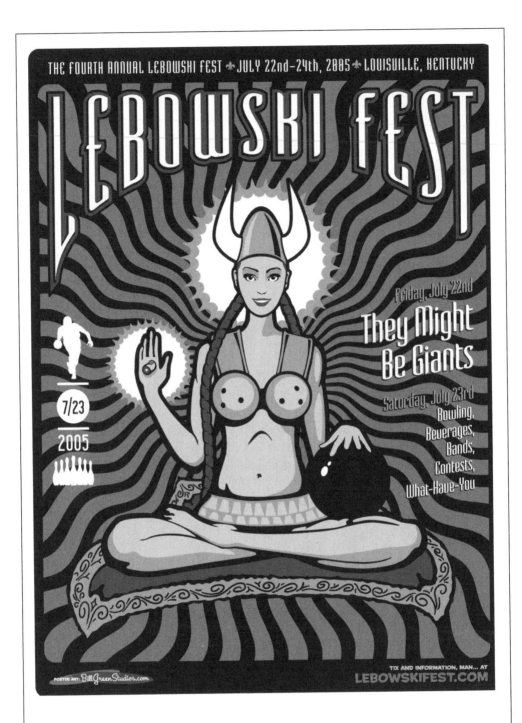

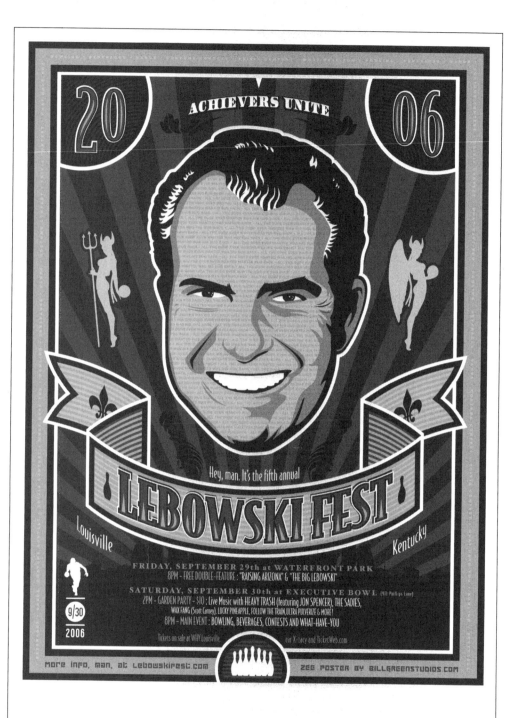

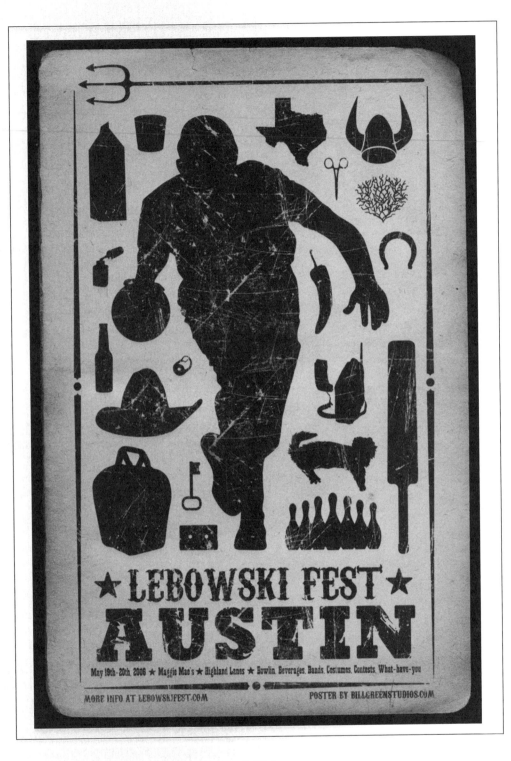

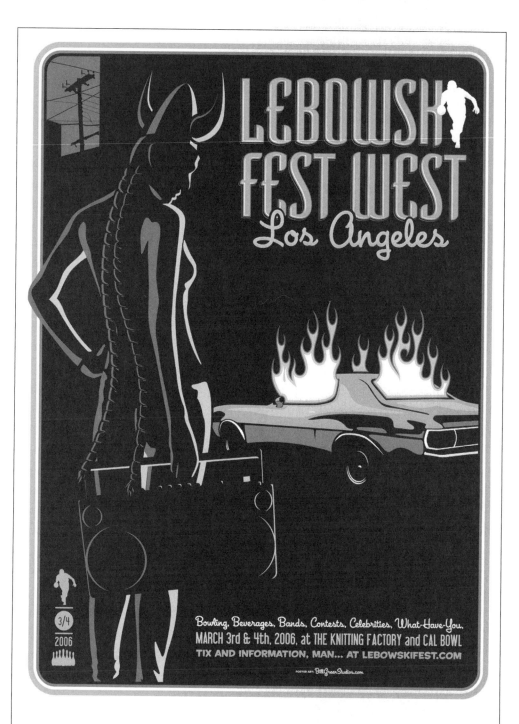

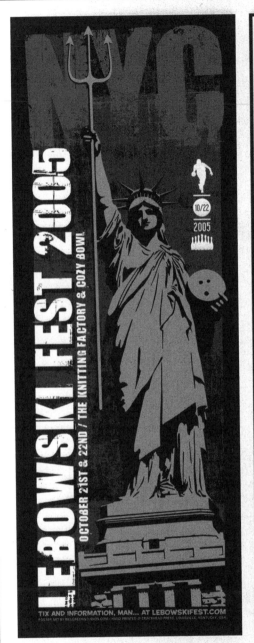

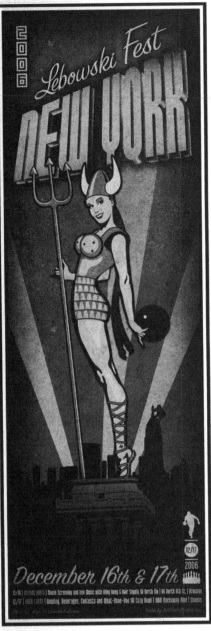

The Fests continue. Look for us in a bowling alley near you. Check out www.LebowskiFest.com for the latest.

CHAPTER SEVEN

REFERENCE MATERIALS. A BY-YOUR-SIDE GUIDE TO WATCHING *THE BIG LEBOWSKI*

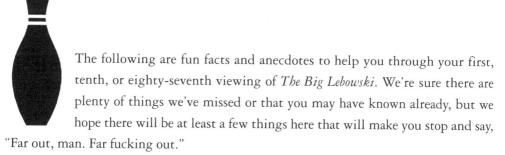

The following are fun facts and anecdotes to help you through your first, tenth, or eighty-seventh viewing of *The Big Lebowski*. We're sure there are plenty of things we've missed or that you may have known already, but we hope there will be at least a few things here that will make you stop and say, "Far out, man. Far fucking out."

The time codes below refer to the film's original DVD release by Polygram. For those of you on the Universal DVD, please add twenty seconds.

00:00:59—In the Stranger's intro, the word *Dude* makes its first of 160 appearances in the film.

00:02:04—Recalling the supermarket scene in *Raising Arizona*, the "Tumbling Tumbleweeds" theme follows the Dude into Ralphs as piped-in Muzak.

00:03:01—The Dude's check is dated September 11, 1991, and, as he's writing it, the first President Bush can be heard on TV in the background declaring, "This aggression will not stand." More than just a bizarre coincidence, this also seems to be a nod to *The Big Sleep*, in which the 9/11 date shows up very early on one of Carmen Sternwood's promissory notes. Also, in the background on the check is an image of a humpback whale, foreshadowing the *Song of the Whale* cassette the Dude listens to in his bathtub later in the film.

00:03:38—To protect himself in this shot, Jeff Bridges is actually dunking his own head in the toilet, pulling the thug's hand along with him.

00:04:15—The Dude says, "Man!" for the first of many times. 174, to be precise.

00:04:38—The Dude holds up the wrong hand to show he's not wearing a wedding ring.

00:06:31—"Roderick Jaynes" is a pseudonym. The Coen brothers actually edited *The Big Lebowski* (and many of their other movies) themselves, with the help of Tricia Cooke, a distinguished film editor who happens to be Ethan's wife.

00:06:34—What's up with that bowling ball? One second it's orange, the next it's green!

00:06:35—This is the first of three seven-ten splits in the movie.

00:07:36—One of *The Big Lebowski*'s seminal lines, the observation that the rug "really tied the room together," was coined by the Coens' friend "Uncle" Pete Exline. (See interview page 97.)

00:07:52—The word *fuck* and its variations are spoken 281 times in the film. Search for "*The*

Big Lebowski Fucking Short Version" on YouTube.com to see all of the movies F-bombs strung together in two minutes and fourteen seconds.

00:08:53—We never get to see the Dude actually bowl: only stretch before a game.

00:09:47—The plaque on the wall reads, ACHIEVER OF THE YEAR, VARIETY CLUBS INTERNATIONAL.

00:10:40—The "Chuck" to whom the Dude refers is the president-for-life of the NRA, Charlton Heston.

00:11:39—In the early 1970s, *Time* magazine actually did produce a set of mirrors just like the one on the Big Lebowski's wall. This scene is also the inspiration for the term *Achiever*, as used to describe a fan of *The Big Lebowski*.

00:13:01—The Dude's character was inspired in part by a longtime friend of the Coen brothers, Jeff Dowd. Dowd's friends gave him the nickname "The Dude" when he was a kid, and it has stuck with him ever since. (See his interview page 89.)

00:13:04—"This aggression will not stand, man," is a riff on the line from President Bush's televised speech in Ralphs in the movie's opening scene. This is just one example of the movie's circular dialogue, in which certain key phrases are picked up by multiple characters and used in different ways.

00:14:38—The floor in the Big Lebowski's mansion is the same as the floor in the Dude's dream sequence later in the film, when he descends the staircase.

00:16:17—That mustachioed bowler in the background is Jeff "The Dude" Dowd.

00:16:42—Ever notice how Walter is always wrong? His dog is actually a terrier, not a Pomeranian.

00:17:14—Smokey is played by Jimmie Dale Gilmore, one of several accomplished musicians with small roles in the film. On a personal level, the Coens are fans and have been spotted at a number of his gigs.

00:18:35—Hollywood Star Lanes, the bowling alley in which the movie's bowling scenes were shot, opened in 1962 and remained Hollywood's only bowling alley for forty years. With a killer jukebox and an open-all-night schedule, it was the late-night bowling hangout of choice for celebrities and locals alike. The last ball thrown at the Hollywood Star Lanes was on August 27, 2002. Soon after, it was demolished to make room for an elementary school. Good night, sweet prince.

00:19:00—The "Pomeranian" walking next to Walter as they exit the bowling alley never actually makes it into the car.

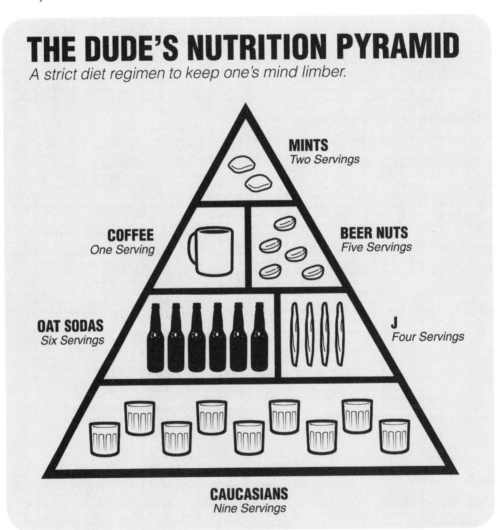

THE DUDE'S NUTRITION PYRAMID
A strict diet regimen to keep one's mind limber.

MINTS
Two Servings

COFFEE
One Serving

BEER NUTS
Five Servings

OAT SODAS
Six Servings

J
Four Servings

CAUCASIANS
Nine Servings

00:20:03—The photo for the poster of Richard Nixon bowling above the Dude's tiki bar was taken in the basement of the White House. Nixon had a small bowling alley installed in the White House during his first term and was an avid bowler.

00:21:02—The Dude consumes his first of nine White Russians. Mark it! Along with the nine White Russians, the Dude downs four beers and one coffee and smokes four joints during the course of the film. The only food he eats is a handful of nuts at the bar and two mints at the funeral home.

00:21:45—The T-shirt Jeff Bridges is wearing in this scene is his own. He also wore the shirt on-screen in *The Fisher King*. The figure on the shirt is Kaoru Betto, known throughout Japan as the Gentleman of Baseball.

00:22:37—This great room scene bears a strong resemblance to the great room scene in *The Big Sleep*, which strongly influenced *The Big Lebowski*.

00:24:50—Take a close look at the Jesus's hand: He's sporting three 300-game rings and, on his pinkie, a coke nail.

00:24:50—The soundtrack to this scene is the Gipsy Kings' Spanish version of "Hotel California," originally written and sung by . . . the fuckin' Eagles!

00:25:28—The lane numbers in this scene are reversed because the film's bowling consultant, Barry Asher, actually threw the ball. He is left-handed and his balls hook to the right, but the Jesus bowls right-handed, and the ball in this shot needed to hook to the left.

00:26:40—A package of birdseed was added to the Jesus's pants in this scene to give his own "package" extra emphasis.

00:27:03—This scene has inspired hours of debate among dedicated Achievers over the question of whom Walter is speaking to when he says, "Life does not stop and start at your convenience, you miserable piece of shit." Donny? The Big Lebowski? Both? Well, Dude, we just don't know.

00:27:47—Donny is constantly being told to "shut the fuck up!" This is a possible reference to Steve Buscemi's character in *Fargo*, who would never shut up.

00:29:23—Side A of the tape the Dude is listening to reads, "Venice Beach League Playoffs 1987." Side B just says "Bob." "Bob" is short for Bob Dylan, who penned "The Man in Me," the song that plays during the Dude's dream sequence. In a nice segue, you can make out "The Man in Me" playing on the Dude's headphones just before he wakes up.

00:31:10—That book on the Dude's coffee table is a Japanese cookbook.

00:33:00—"Dude here" is also how Jeff "The Dude" Dowd on occasion answers his cell phone in real life.

00:35:54—After numerous failed attempts to film the Dude throwing the ringer from his car, Jeff Bridges finally suggested the idea of filming this sequence in reverse. It worked! Also, the wooden planks that cover the bridge were added for filming because the Coens liked the sound the car made as it passed over them.

00:36:00—More Creedence! The song playing during this scene is CCR's "Run Through the Jungle."

00:36:34—Walter's limp in this scene is no act. John Goodman actually hurt his ankle while riding his Harley a couple of days before this scene was shot.

00:37:35—Phone's ringin', Dude.

00:37:38—*Aitz chaim he* means "It is the tree of life" in Yiddish.

00:41:51—The Dude's answering machine message has inspired countless imitations. The full message is: "The Dude is not in. Leave a message after the beep. Takes a minute."

00:42:55—In certain circles of Lebowski scholarship, it's believed that Maude as an artist is loosely based on prominent feminist artist Carolee Schneemann.

00:42:57—The sound that introduces Maude's flying descent into the scene is just like that of a bowling ball when it first touches wood on its way down the lane.

00:43:03—This is not Julianne Moore's first time flying on-screen: She had previous harness experience from her work in *Jurassic Park: The Lost World*.

00:44:07—The painting of a giant pair of scissors on the wall foreshadows the giant pair of scissors that will later chase the Dude in his dream sequence.

00:45:47—The actual jumpsuit worn by Uli in this scene is on display at Lebowski Fest World Headquarters. It's been autographed by Peter Stormare.

00:46:02—Bunny's friend Sherry is played by legendary porn star Asia Carrera. She later reported that during filming, the Coens were impressed that she could deliver her lines as comfortably with her shirt off as she did with her shirt on. Asia is also a member of MENSA.

00:48:18—The sandals Jeff Bridges is wearing are part of his personal wardrobe. They're called jellies, and he acquired them during the filming of *White Squall*.

00:49:58—This scene is the collective favorite of all the cast members. The Dude's "ums" and "uhs" might seem spontaneous, but they were all carefully scripted by the Coens.

00:52:42—Johnie's, where this scene was shot, is no longer a working diner. It now opens solely for films shooting on location.

00:53:30—Lu, the name on the waitress's name tag, is the actress's real name. Lu Elrod is an accomplished ventriloquist and performer, and she is also a tenured professor in the University of California system.

00:54:17—This shot of the Dude's ten toes forms a nice counterpoint to the severed toe in the previous scene. It also provides an ominous echo to the Big Lebowski's line, "Any further harm to Bunny will be visited *tenfold* upon your head."

00:54:27—The Dude is listening to *Song of the Whale: Ultimate Relaxation*—a wink to the whale image on his checks in the opening scene.

00:54:55—That's a cricket bat Torsten Voges is using to smash up the Dude's apartment. No nihilist would be caught dead with a Louisville Slugger.

00:55:12—The nice marmot is actually a ferret. Just ask any park ranger.

00:55:13—The shortest of the nihilists is played by Flea, renowned bassist of the Red Hot Chili Peppers.

00:55:18—To film this scene, the filmmakers created a marmot prop on a stick. The marmot-on-a-stick was controlled by a power drill on the other side of the tub wall.

00:55:25—That's a Scrubbing Bubbles toy on the side of the Dude's tub, a nice vintage find by the production designer.

00:59:05—Gary the Bartender is played by Peter "Goose" Siragusa. Goose has acted in three Coen brothers films, but this is the only time his scene has not ended up on the cutting-room floor.

01:00:00—Sam Elliott's phrasing of "Sometimes you eat the bar . . ." is based on Fess Parker's, a TV star of the fifties and sixties who used to say *bar* for *bear* in just the same way.

01:00:56—The Stranger first exits in one direction and then turns and goes the other way. The false start came initially from Sam Elliott, but when he asked the Coens which way he should go, one of them replied, "Fuck, I don't know, man. Go both ways!" As Elliott put it, "The wind caught me."

01:01:10—Maude is the only character in the film whom the Dude allows to call him Jeffrey.

01:06:28—The subject of little Larry's homework is the Louisiana Purchase. As you can see, he's a fuckin' dunce. Flunkin' social studies.

01:06:30—His teacher's name is Ms. Jamtoss. More than one Achiever has come in costume to a Lebowski Fest dressed as Ms. Jamtoss.

01:06:50—Jack Kehler developed the dance for his cycle under the guidance of Bill and Jacqui Landrum, the choreographers who also orchestrated the movie's two dream sequences.

01:07:51—*Branded* was an actual TV show, on the air from 1965 to 1966.

01:08:14—Jack Kehler, who plays Marty the Landlord, said that at the end of his cycle he did the same trademark fist-pump gesture that he did at the end of his first scene with the Dude. To his great disappointment, it didn't make the final cut.

01:11:00—This scene with the homework was inspired by real-life events. The Coens' friend Peter Exline and Exline's friend Lew Abernathy actually found homework and fast food wrappers after police retrieved Exline's stolen car. In hopes of providing the miscreant with a life lesson, they put the homework and the hamburger wrappers in separate baggies and paid him a visit. (See chapter 3 for the full story.)

01:12:20—In the edited-for-TV version of the film, Goodman's line "Do you see what happens when you fuck a stranger in the ass?" is overdubbed as, "Do you see what happens when you find a stranger in the Alps?"

01:12:28—During the filming of this scene, John Goodman was never told that the Coens had bought out the neighborhood for the night. Goodman spent the whole shoot afraid that his shouting would wake all the neighbors.

01:14:22—On this second incursion into the Dude's apartment, Treehorn's thugs have actually swapped shirts from their first visit.

01:19:12—The Dude may have occupied various administration buildings, but he wasn't a math major. Ten percent of half a million is actually $50,000, not $5,000.

01:20:20—The song here, "Just Dropped In (to See What Condition My Condition Was

In)," is sung by Kenny Rogers and the First Edition (long before his better-known hits "Lady," "The Gambler," and "Islands in the Stream").

01:22:40—To lighten the mood while filming this shot, the chorine dancers actually tucked bunches of black crepe hair into their panties between their legs to surprise Jeff Bridges as he passed beneath them. The Dude's smile here is more than just fine acting!

01:24:01—The song the Dude is half singing, half mumbling here is the actual *Branded* theme song.

01:24:35—Ron Kuby, one of the lawyers the Dude references here as his attorney, is the name of an attorney who hosts a successful morning radio program in New York City. Bill Kunstler, the other lawyer to whom the Dude makes reference, is an attorney whose career as a radical, peace-activist lawyer spanned more than fifty years.

01:28:25—Out of all the accomplishments that the Dude lists here to Maude, being a roadie for Metallica is the only one that Jeff Dowd claims did not actually happen. All of the others, he asserts, happened in his life—up to and including helping a "lady friend" to conceive.

01:29:28—Jeff Bridges once said that his preferred drink is not a White Russian, but vodka on the rocks, which he refers to as just a Russian.

01:29:35—The Dude is not exactly a light reader: The book on his nightstand is Jean-Paul Sartre's *Being and Nothingness*, one of several references to existentialism in the film. Another is the name of Sam Elliott's character, the Stranger.

01:34:17—The fact that Peter Stormare's character orders the lingonberry pancakes could be taken as a humorous reference to his previous Coen brothers role as Gaear Grimsrud in *Fargo*, in which he has a constant craving for pancakes.

01:34:38—This scene at the diner is the only scene in the movie without the Dude. Also, the nine-toed woman on the left is noted singer-songwriter Aimee Mann.

01:36:35—Sandy Koufax is one of the most highly respected baseball pitchers of all time, revered in his day not only for his skills on the mound but also for being one of the first Jewish players to crack the major leagues. As for Moses . . . him you have probably heard of.

01:36:53—Bunny's license plate reads "LAPIN," which is French for "rabbit."

01:38:06—Paraquat is one of the most widely used herbicides in the world. Thus, to say, "you human paraquat" does not make much sense. Which only makes it that much funnier.

01:39:22—This is the only bowling frame in the film in which Donny does not bowl a strike, foreshadowing his coming death in the next sequence.

01:39:50—What the Dude is applying to his fingernail here is not nail polish; it's liquid skin or liquid Band-Aid, used by bowlers to cover blisters. An actual bandage would be too thick and would impede their ability to get their fingers in and out of the holes.

01:40:16—The Jesus and Liam define the word *team:* They remain color-coordinated here, as they were in their first appearance.

01:40:52—The neon starbursts on the exterior of the bowling alley were added by the production designers for filming. They were not actually part of the original bowling alley, but the owners of the Hollywood Star Lanes liked them so much that they left them up after the filming wrapped.

01:44:00—*The Big Lebowski* is Steve Buscemi's fifth Coen brothers film, and he has been killed in three of them. Each time he's killed, his remains get progressively smaller, from a full corpse in *Miller's Crossing*, to being run through a wood chipper in *Fargo*, to being cremated and sprinkled on the Dude in *The Big Lebowski*.

01:47:50—The phrase "Good night, sweet prince," with which Walter concludes his eulogy, is a quotation from Horatio in Shakespeare's *Hamlet*.

01:48:53—Notice the random torso in the upper right corner of this frame.

01:49:50—An oat soda is a beer.

01:51:04—The Coens made Sam Elliott do more than a dozen takes of the Stranger's final monologue. Finally growing frustrated, Elliott asked them, "What the fuck is up, boys?" The Coens replied, "We got it on take eight. We just like seeing you do it."

01:52:11—The bowler in this frame is Barry Asher, the legendary pro bowler who served as the film's on-set bowling consultant. He bowls the movie's first and final balls.

Nice Marmot

Marmots are usually the size of a house cat and include fourteen species, among them the groundhog, woodchuck, and prairie dog. The marmot is only found in the Northern Hemisphere and was the primary carrier of the bubonic plague during several outbreaks, not the rat as commonly believed.

¿Parla Usted Achiever?
An English-Achiever Translation Guide

Since most of the Internet translation websites have not yet added Achiever to the list of languages they translate to and from (although we're confident they will soon), we've put together a guide of our own. Whether you're a die-hard Achiever looking to sharpen your skills or a baffled loved one hoping to find out what the hell your Achiever is talking about, this guide should help.

English: I told you this was gonna happen.
Achiever: They finally did it. They killed my fuckin' car.

English: I agree. *see also* "It's settled."
Achiever: Does the pope shit in the woods?

English: It's not really that expensive.
Achiever: It is our most modestly priced receptacle.

English: I don't give a shit. *or* This does not affect the Lord and Savior.
Achiever: It don't matter to Jesus.

English: What do you mean you can't make it?
Achiever: What's this day-of-rest shit?

English: I'll see you on [*insert day*].
Achiever: [*in Quintana accent*] You gotta date [*insert day*], baby!

English: That person is exceptionally talented.
Achiever: Worthy fucking adversary. *see also* "That creep can roll."

English: I don't believe him/her.
Achiever: This guy fuckin' walks. I've never been more certain of anything in my life.

English: Well done, sir.
Achiever: Fabulous stuff.

English: Well, aren't they fancy now?
Achiever: How're you gonna keep 'em down on the farm once they've seen Karl Hungus?

English: This doesn't concern me.
Achiever: I'm sorry your stepmother is a nympho.

English: Be quiet.
Achiever: Shut the fuck up, Donny! *or* Please lower your voice, sir, this is a family restaurant.

English: It's settled.
Achiever: Mark it! *see also* "I Agree"

English: Goodbye.
Achiever: Take 'er easy.

English: Nice shirt/pants/outfit.
Achiever: I like yer style, Dude.

English: You are not very nice. *or* A response when someone inflicts unwarranted bodily harm on you.
Achiever: Fucking fascist!

English: Didn't you know that?
Achiever: Hasn't that ever occurred to you, man . . . sir?

English: You're not doing that right.
Achiever: Dude, are you fucking this up?

English: I'll take you up on that offer.
Achiever: I'm just gonna go find a cash machine.

English: I didn't know you knew so much about wildlife.
Achiever: What are you, a fucking park ranger now?

English: Sex
Achiever: Fixing the cable *or* coitus. *see also* "natural zesty enterprise"

English: That's inappropriate.
Achiever: Over the line!

English: You're upsetting me.
Achiever: You are entering a world of pain.

English: Can I borrow a dollar?
Achiever: I gotta feed the monkey.

English: Does this belong to you?
Achiever: Is this your homework, Larry?

English: That's expensive.
Achiever: Just because we are bereaved does not make us saps!

English: I was wondering about the same thing.
Achiever: This is our concern, Dude.

English: I did not know that.
Achiever: That had not occurred to me, Dude.

And they say he ran away . . . *Branded*!

The television show for which Arthur Digby Sellers wrote the "bulk of the series," *Branded* is an actual show that ran from 1965 to 1966. It was created by Larry Cohen. The plot summary is that in the 1880s, West Point graduate Jason McCord travels the country trying to prove he's no coward after being thrown out of the army.

English: It's basically the same thing.

Achiever: Are we gonna split hairs here?

English: I disagree with what you just said.

Achiever: I'm sorry, I wasn't listening. *or* Yeah, well, that's just like . . . your opinion, man.

English: What do you do for a living?

Achiever: Are you employed, sir?

English: I really like that [*noun*].

Achiever: That [*noun*] really ties the room together.

English: Double-cross somebody.

Achiever: Fuck a stranger in the ass.

English: I'm not sure you realize the consequences of your actions.

Achiever: You're killing your father, Larry.

English: Competent, capable.

Achiever: Not exactly a lightweight.

I can get you a toe

According to Dr. Raymond G. Hart, MD, MPH, the executive director at Kleinert Institute for Hand and Microsurgery in Louisville, Kentucky, a severed toe can last up to six hours and

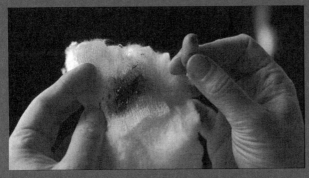

still be reattached successfully. If the toe is placed in a baggie and put on ice, it may last up to twenty-four and possibly even thirty hours. Depending on the quality and type, the nail polish may last as long as ten days before it begins to degrade.

English: I like those. They're all right with me.
Achiever: Those are good burgers, Dude.

English: We're on top of it.
Achiever: They got us working in shifts!

English: Keep it legitimate.
Achiever: No funny schtuff.

English: That's perfect.
Achiever: That's a Swiss fucking watch.

English: It didn't go as well as we hoped.
Achiever: Dude's car got a little dinged up.

English: It's a complete disaster!
Achiever: The goddamned plane has crashed into the mountain!

English: We have received some new information.
Achiever: New shit has come to light.

English: I won't tolerate any more of this.
Achiever: I will not abide another toe.

English: I can get that done for you.
Achiever: I can get you a toe by three o'clock this afternoon.

English: I'll go the extra mile.
Achiever: With nail polish.

English: Phone's ringing.
Achiever: Phone's ringing, Dude.

English: Feminine, ladylike.
Achiever: Strongly vaginal.

English: You win some, you lose some.
Achiever: Strikes and gutters, ups and downs.

English: You really know what you're doing.
Achiever: You mix a helluva Caucasian, Jackie.

English: How did I get myself in this situation?
Achiever: All the Dude ever wanted was his rug back.

English: I can see clearly now. The rain is gone.
Achiever: A few burgers, a few beers, a few laughs . . . our fuckin' troubles are over.

English: There's a lot to keep track of here.
Achiever: Lotta ins, lotta outs, lotta what have yous. *also* Lotta strands in old Duder's head.

English: That's against the rules.
Achiever: That ain't legal, either.

English: It all worked out okay in the end.
Achiever: And we do enter the next round-robin.

In The Parlance of Our Times

A glossary of terms and preferred nomenclatures for all things Lebowski

abide *v* To endure, sustain, or withstand without yielding or submitting. Such as the Dude does after having his head shoved into a toilet, his rug peed on, his bungalow burgled, and his car dinged up. I don't know about you, but we take comfort in that.

Achiever *n* The preferred nomenclature for a fan of *The Big Lebowski*. Derived from the Little Lebowski Urban Achievers, inner-city children of promise, but without the necessary means for a higher education. And proud we are of all of them.

amateur *n* Someone who has never seen *The Big Lebowski* or doesn't "get it." Someone who is obviously not a golfer. *also known as* **fucking amateurs**

beaver picture *n* An "adult" film known to have a ludicrous story line and feature friends coming over to use the shower and German cable repairmen. You can imagine where it goes from here. *see also* **Logjammin'**

bum *n* Someone who is unemployed. Somebody the square community won't give a shit about. Well, aren't ya?

Caucasian *n* An alternate name for the beverage known as the White Russian.

Chinaman *n* We're not talking about the guy who built the railroads here, we're talking about someone who took Mr. Lebowski's legs in Korea. Also, Dude, *Chinaman* is not the preferred nomenclature. *Asian American*, please.

coitus *n* Sex; the physical act of love. Can be a natural, zesty enterprise. Sometimes known as **banging**, to use the parlance of our times.

Dude *n* A man for his time and place. Someone who takes it easy for all us sinners. *also known as* **Duder**, **His Dudeness**, or **El Duderino** if you're not into the whole brevity thing.

fascist *n* A person who is dictatorial or has extreme right-wing views. Often, a real reactionary.

goldbricker *n* A person who shirks responsibility; a parasite who lives on the wealth of others. *see also* **Mr. Lebowski (the cripple)**

marmot *n* The preferred nomenclature for any land mammal resembling a ferret. Keeping this type of animal within city limits, that ain't legal either, Dude.

micturate *v* To pee or urinate, as on one's rug.

nihilist *n* One who believes in nothing. Pastimes include techno-pop music, severing toes, marmot wrangling, threatening castration, and passing out in pools. May cause exhaustion.

oat soda *n* American pilsner ale; beer; *see also* **Miller Lite**

paraquat *n* An herbicide.

pederast *n* A child molester; one who exposes himself to eight-year-olds. *see also* **Jesus Quintana**

prior restraint *n* Judicial prevention of a statement or other expression from being published. Which, Dude, the Supreme Court has roundly rejected.

ringer *n* A bag whose implied contents are different than its actual contents. Could be filled with dirty undies or "the whites" to simulate equivalent weight of a specified amount of money. The ringer cannot look empty.

roll *v* To bowl. <Fucking Quintana—that creep can ~, man.> Thus, if you're **rollin' rocks**, you're having a good night.

Shabbos *n* The Jewish day of rest. This means you don't drive a car, you don't ride in a car, you don't handle money, you don't turn on the oven, and you sure as shit don't fucking roll! One who is "Shomer Shabbos" actively observes this day.

special lady *n* A girlfriend. Not to be confused with a **lady friend**, who is someone you may just be helping to conceive, man.

stonewall *v* To stall, refuse to cooperate. Such as Little Larry did to Walter.

trophy wife *n* A wife who is for show only, usually an attractive young strumpet such as Bunny Lebowski.

throwing rocks *v* Bowling well. The term for three strikes in a row is a **turkey**. Four strikes in a row is called a **four bagger**.

Vietnam *n* A world of pain, where Walter watched his buddies die facedown in the muck so that we could enjoy our basic freedoms and family restaurants.

Is that some kind of Eastern thing? Foreign titles of *The Big Lebowski*

- *A Nagy Lebowski*—Hungary
- *El Gran Lebowski*—Argentina, Spain
- *Il Grande Lebowski*—Italy
- *O Grande Lebowski*—Portugal
- *Le Grand Lebowski*—France

The Big Lebowski Ultimate Soundtrack

The CD released as the movie's "official soundtrack" in no way did justice to the amazing collection of music the Coens and their musical collaborator, T-Bone Burnett, assembled for the film. It didn't even have any Creedence.

Unfortunately we can't right that travesty. But, as we all know, the Dude minds. So we've put together the following list of every piece of music in the film.

"Tumbling Tumbleweeds"
Written by Bob Nolan
Performed by Sons of the Pioneers

"The Man in Me"
Written and performed by Bob Dylan

"Mucha Muchacha"
Written by Juan Garcia Esquivel
Performed by Esquivel

"I Hate You"
Written by Gary Burger, David Havlicek, Roger Johnston, Thomas E. Shaw, and Larry
    Spangler
Performed by Monks

"Her Eyes Are a Blue Million Miles"
Written by Don Vliet
Performed by Captain Beefheart

"Requiem in D Minor"
Written by W. A. Mozart
Performed by the Slovak Philharmonic Orchestra and Choir

"Hotel California"

Written by Don Henley, Glenn Frey, and Don Felder (the fuckin' Eagles)

Performed by the Gipsy Kings

"Gluck Das Mir Verblieb" from the opera *Die Tote Stadt*

Written and conducted by Erich Wolfgang Korngold

Performed by Ilona Steingruber, Anton Dermota, and the Austrian State Radio
    Orchestra

"Run Through the Jungle"

Written by John Fogerty

Performed by Creedence Clearwater Revival

"Behave Yourself"

Written by Booker T. Jones, Steve Cropper, Al Jackson Jr., and Lewis Steinberg

Performed by Booker T. & MG's

"Walking Song"

Written and performed by Meredith Monk

"Traffic Boom"

Written and performed by Piero Piccioni

"Standing on the Corner"

Written by Frank Loesser

Performed by Dean Martin

"Tammy"

Written by Ray Evans and Jay Livingston

Performed by Debbie Reynolds

Songs of the Whale: Ultimate Relaxation

Written and performed by the humpback whales

Produced by Roger Payne

"My Mood Swings"
Written by Elvis Costello and Cait O'Riordan
Performed by Elvis Costello

"We Venerate Thy Cross"
Traditional
Performed by the Rustavi Choir

"Looking out My Back Door"
Written by John Fogerty
Performed by Creedence Clearwater Revival

"Pictures at an Exhibition"
Written by Modest Mussorgsky
Conducted by Sir Colin Davis
Performed by the Royal Concertgebouw Orchestra

"Oye Como Va"
Written by Tito Puente
Performed by Santana

"Ataypura"
Written by Moises Vivanco
Performed by Yma Sumac

"Lujon"
Written and performed by Henry Mancini

"Piacere Sequence"
Written and performed by Teo Usuelli

"Just Dropped In (to See What Condition My Condition Was In)"
Written by Mickey Newbury
Performed by Kenny Rogers and the First Edition

Branded Theme Song
Written by Alan Alch and Dominic Frontiere

"Peaceful Easy Feeling"
Written by Jack Tempchin
Performed by the Eagles

"Viva Las Vegas"
Written by Doc Pomus and Mort Shuman
Performed by Big Johnson (Bunny's ride home) and Shawn Colvin (end credits)

"I Got It Bad (and That Ain't Good)"
Written by Duke Ellington and Paul Francis Webster
Performed by Nina Simone

"Stamping Ground"
Written by Louis Hardin (aka Moondog)
Performed by Moondog

"Wie Glauben" (Nihilists' Theme Song)
Written and performed by Carter Burwell

"Dead Flowers"
Written by Mick Jagger and Keith Richards
Performed by Townes Van Zandt

LEBOWSKI
LOCATIONS

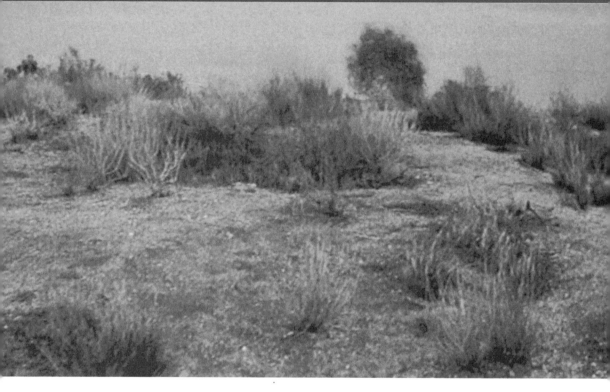

Tumblin' Tumbleweeds

The very first shot in the film, the tumbleweed climbing up the hill, was filmed in Pear Blossom, California, and was actually the very last shot filmed. It was then (presumably) merged with the shot of the L.A. cityscape. The other locales featured in the opening include the Benito's taco stand that used to be on 3rd and Edinburgh (the first of several uniquely Southern California businesses featured), a freeway overpass, an empty Hollywood street (Sunset Boulevard, of course), and a deserted beach at night.

The following list of locations used in the filming of *The Big Lebowski* was assembled by L.A. native Pat Evans, also known as Location Freak (a name he self-applied). Pat is a true Achiever and quite a brother shamus: He spent countless hours scouring the streets of Los Angeles to track down these locations (but, no, he does not drive a blue Volkswagen Beetle). Thanks, Pat. You went out and achieved anyway. Proud we are of all of you!

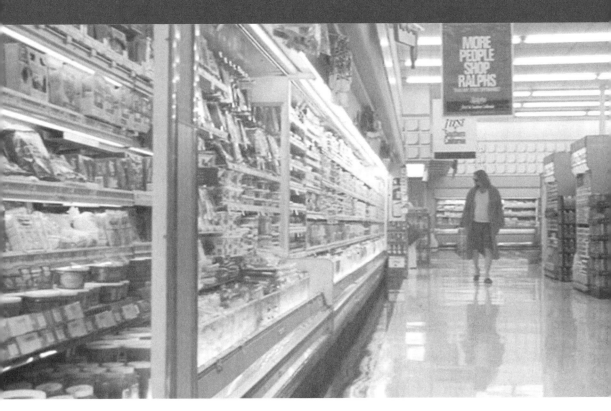

Ralphs

Our first visual of Jeff "The Dude" Lebowski is in the second-largest of our SoCal chains, Ralphs grocery store. You can't throw a rock in L.A. without hitting a Ralphs, which has made it difficult so far to determine exactly which Ralphs was used for filming, but as we know from speaking with Robin Jones (who played the Checkout Girl), it's somewhere on the streets of Pasadena.

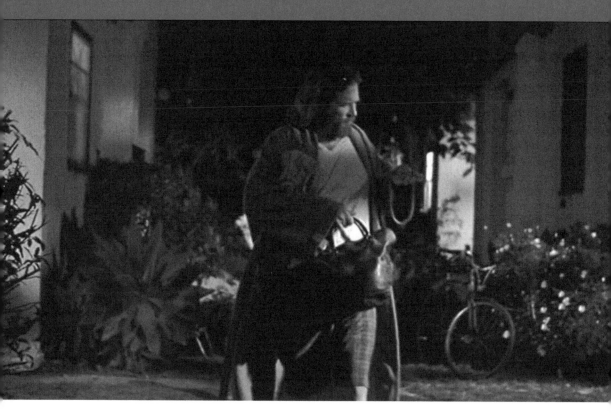

The Dude's Bungalow
Venezia Avenue, Venice

After procuring his half and half, the Dude heads back to his ramshackle Venice bungalow. The exteriors of the bungalow and street were actually filmed in Venice, on Venezia Avenue. I shouldn't even have to say this, but I will: This is a private residence, man. If you go and have a look, do not disturb the residents! Stay on the sidewalk. Don't ring any doorbells or peek in any windows.

For the completist, the interior of the bungalow was filmed at a studio in West Hollywood, located at 1011 North Fuller Avenue.

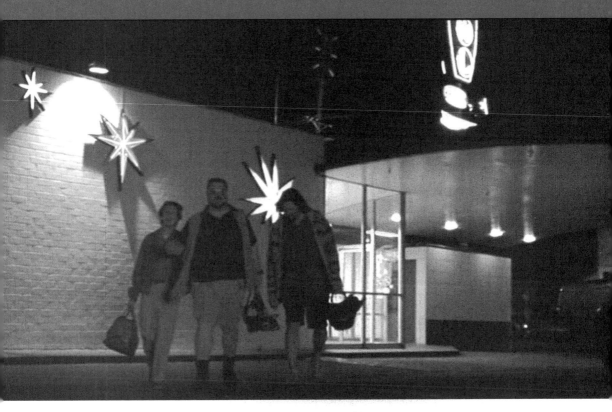

Bowling Alley
Hollywood Star Lanes, 5227 Santa Monica Boulevard, Los Angeles

Tragically, the main Lebowski location (and prime example of Googie architecture), the great Hollywood Star Lanes, has closed for good. The L.A. school board, in its infinite wisdom, purchased the plot and demolished the building to make way for an elementary school. Knowing the neighborhood pretty well (I live right down the street from Hollywood Star Lanes), I have to say this is a patently ridiculous idea. Or maybe I'm underestimating the average parents' desire to have their child exposed to strip clubs, seedy bars, and violent lunatics (who make up a large percentage of my neighbors).

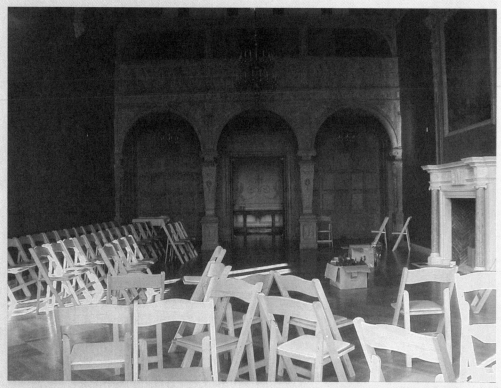

Lebowski Mansion
Greystone Mansion, 905 Loma Vista, Beverly Hills

The Dude confronts the "other" Jeffrey Lebowski in his elegant Pasadena mansion. This was actually two different locations. The interiors were shot at the historic Greystone Mansion in Beverly Hills, which has been featured in numerous other films including the catastrophic *Batman & Robin*, where it served as Wayne Manor. The interior of the house is not generally open to the public, but you can see the fountain where Bunny crashes her sports car in front of the mansion. The other exterior scene, where the Dude first encounters Bunny, was filmed at a residence on Charing Cross Road, also in Beverly Hills.

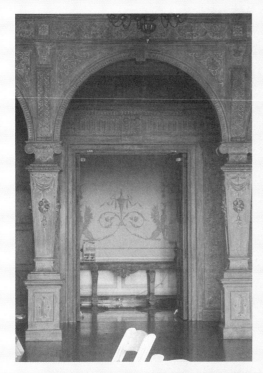
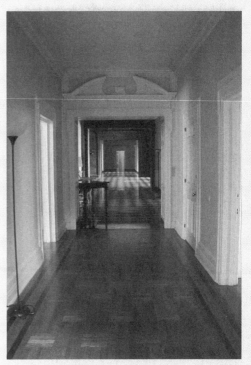
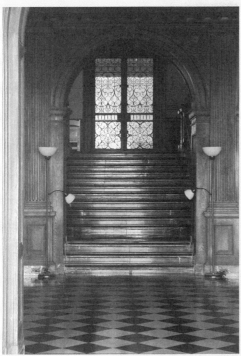
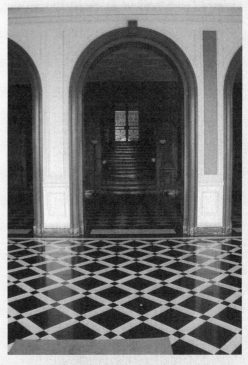

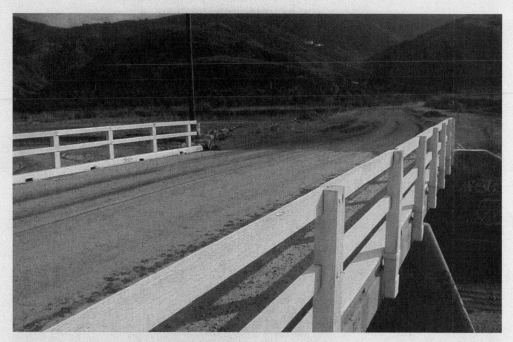

The Wooden Bridge
Torrey Road at Santa Clara River, Piru

Just outside of the tiny hamlet of Piru, California, in the Santa Clara River Valley (not Simi, as implied in the film; the Simi Valley road sign is a prop), lies the wooden bridge where the Dude and Walter hopelessly mangle the ransom drop. This also marks the spot where the Dude's car suffers the first of several incidents of damage, crashing into a tele-

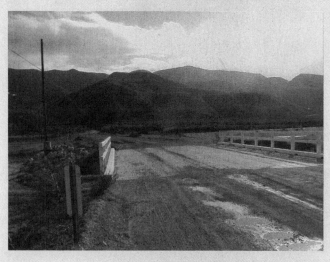

phone pole as stray bullets from Walter's Uzi pelt the back end and blow out a tire. This location is not the middle of nowhere, but it is close. Incidentally, the bridge is not actually wooden. Planks were laid over the top for the shoot.

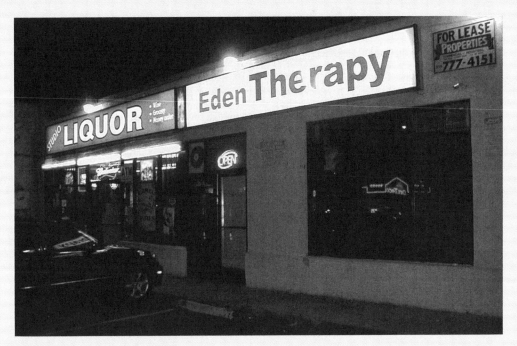

Sobchak Security
6757 Santa Monica Boulevard, Los Angeles

The Dude picks up Walter (replete with brown-paper-wrapped Uzi and undie-filled ringer) outside the storefront for Sobchak Security, Walter's business. Located in a strip mall, this is also a stone's throw from the late Hollywood Star Lanes. And like the bowling alley, this is a very seedy section of Santa Monica Boulevard. Use extreme caution.

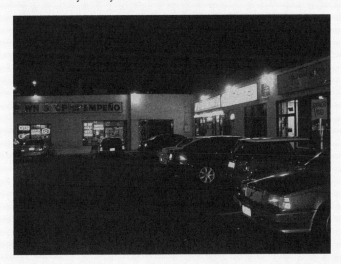

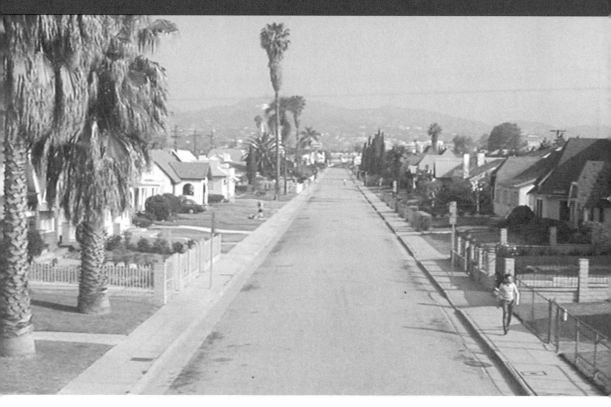

The Jesus Walk of Shame
North Kenmore Avenue, Los Angeles

In this flashback sequence we see John Turturro's pederast bowler Jesus Quintana making the rounds to explain his "checkered past" to his new neighbors, presumably as a result of Megan's Law.

This residential street in the shadow of Griffith Park is not too far from the former Hollywood Star Lanes. Once again, if you are going to have a look, go no farther than the sidewalk. Have a quick gander, then move it along. Don't be un-Dude, man.

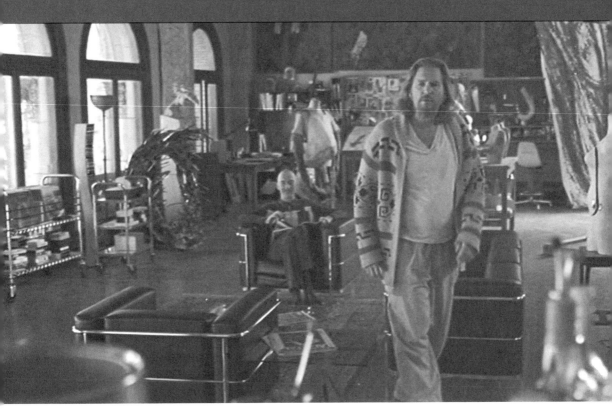

Maude's Loft
Palace Theater, 630 South Broadway, Downtown Los Angeles

The Dude finally meets up with the mysterious fluxus artist Maude Lebowski in her spacious downtown loft, where she literally swoops down upon him, brushes flailing, wearing a leather harness and nothing else. Interesting to note is the abundance of Bang and Olufsen products Maude possesses, from the TV (on which she displays *Logjammin'*) to the nifty horizontal CD changer in the background and the sleek telephone used by Knox Harrington in a later scene. Her couch and chairs look to be of Danish origin as well. Apparently fluxus artists have a penchant for Scandinavian design.

The loft resides above the Palace Theater in downtown L.A., I believe on the second floor. Obviously you can only view the exterior, but if you want to see it, there it is. It's not the greatest neighborhood, so if you go there make it on a weekday afternoon. Preferably in a group.

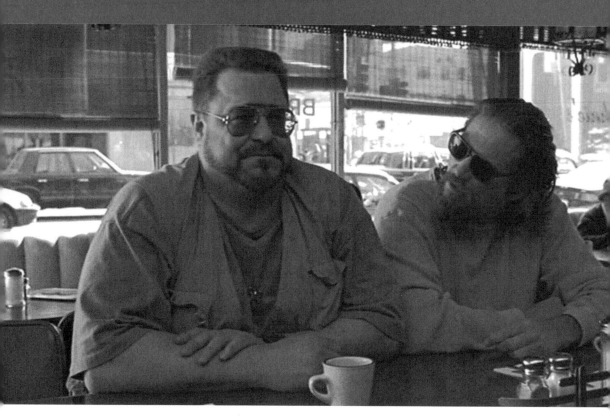

Family Restaurant
Johnie's Coffee Shop, Fairfax & Wilshire, Los Angeles

Another example of Googie architecture, Johnie's has long since closed and is used only as a filming location. It is here that Walter attempts to dispel the notion that the severed toe received by the Big Lebowski and subsequently passed along to the Dude belongs to Bunny. He then proceeds to loudly vocalize his right to free speech, peppering it with Vietnam jargon. All of this to the chagrin of the waitress, the other diners, and the Dude, who leaves in frustration.

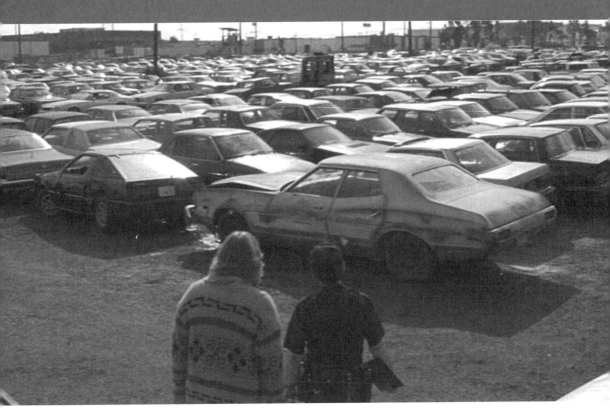

Auto Circus
Location Unknown

The Dude reclaims his vehicle at this auto yard in the North Hollywood area (as depicted in the film). Where exactly? I am not sure. But I did check with the boys in the crime lab, and apparently they have four more detectives working on the case. In shifts.

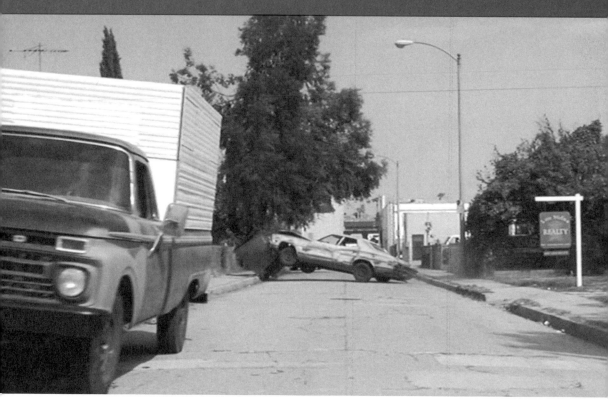

Creedence Crash
La Mirada Avenue, Hollywood

In the post-medical-examination, blue-Volkswagon-Bug-pursuit, roach-in-lap, beer-spilling Dumpster crash scene, the Dude is driving up Cahuenga Boulevard in Hollywood and makes a left onto La Mirada Avenue, heading toward Vine Street when he crashes. The houses on the south side of the street are fenced off. Apparently this is the second Lebowski location that is to become (partially anyway) affected by the building of a new school. In this case it appears to be some sort of private Christian school. Anyway, there it is. The neighborhood is a little scummy, so be advised.

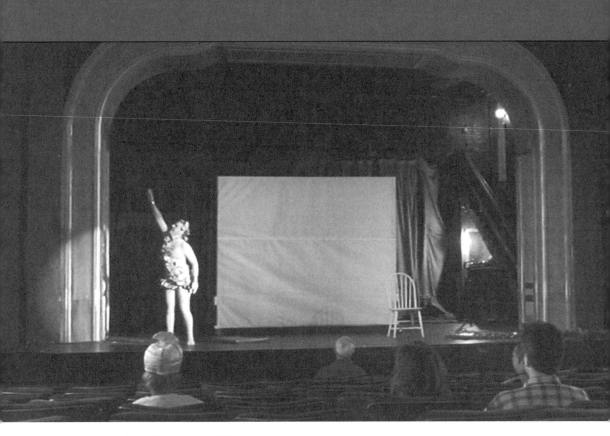

Fountain Street Theater
Palace Theater, 630 South Broadway, Downtown Los Angeles

This scene features Marty the landlord performing his dance quintet ("You know, my cycle . . ."), which the Dude promised to attend earlier in the film. To me, this is one of the shining moments of the film, with Jack Kehler in an inspired turn as a man driven to dance despite the dual handicap of 1) being sadly out of shape; and 2) having no talent. This was filmed in the same building as Maude's apartment, but on a different floor. Marty refers to it as Crane Jackson's Fountain Street Theatre, which may or may not be a reference to the old Theatre Rapport at 1277 North Wilton, near Fountain. The late actor-producer Crane Jackson was apparently active in productions there in the early nineties, the time period of the film. Interestingly, when Jackson first arrived in L.A. in the late sixties, he converted a bowling alley into a stage theater. Coincidence?

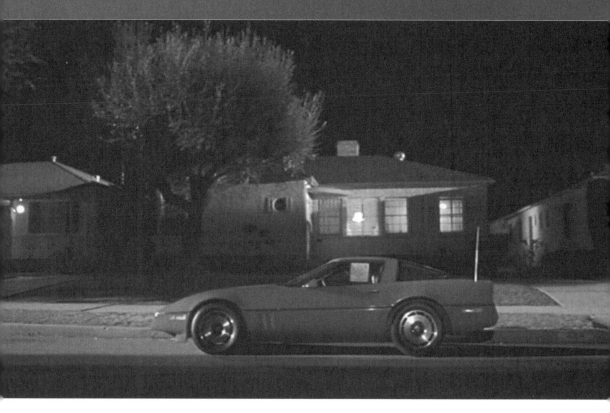

Little Larry's House
Stearns Avenue, Fairfax District, Los Angeles

Next the Dude, Walter, and Donny arrive at the home of Little Larry Sellers. Situated in a nice, quiet residential neighborhood in the Fairfax area (not on Radford in North Hollywood), it's no wonder John Goodman was reticent about shouting obscenities full-volume at three in the morning in the middle of the street while smashing a new Corvette with a crowbar.

Here the Dude's car suffers another round of abuse, this time at the hands of the enraged Corvette owner. Other than being the historic site of this extraordinary display of howling bombast, the house and street are rather unremarkable.

Afterward, Walter and Donny can be seen munching In-N-Out Burgers (another SoCal chain) in the Dude's car as the Dude stares morosely through the spot where his windshield used to be.

Once again, be respectful if you visit this or any of the neighborhoods on this list. Stay out of the yards. And for God's sake, do not yell anything! No one will think you are clever.

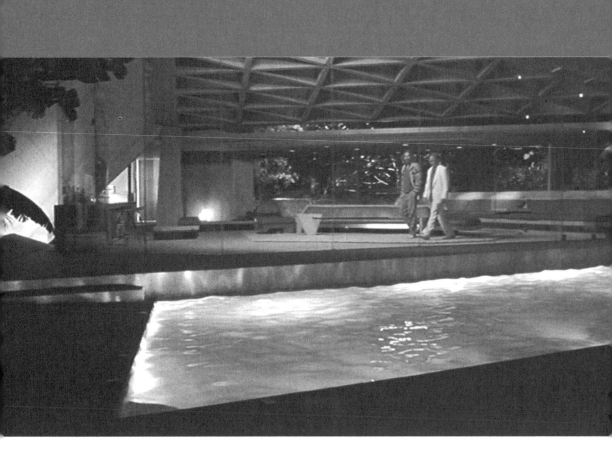

Treehorn's Pad
Sheats/Goldstein Residence, Benedict Canyon

The Dude takes another turn for the worse after a mickey is slipped into his White Russian while he's at the porn magnate's swank Malibu beach house.

The funky, angular glass-and-concrete interior was actually filmed in the Benedict Canyon of Beverly Hills at the Sheats/Goldstein house. Designed by the renowned architect (and, wouldn't you know it, the father of Googie) John Lautner, it has been featured in a few movies, including the James Bond film *Diamonds Are Forever*.

The exterior beach-party scene was on Zuma Beach.

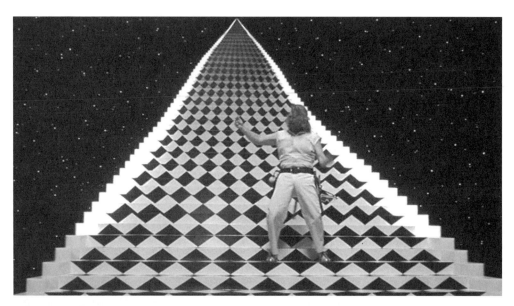

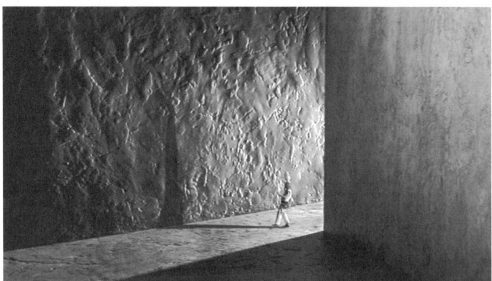

Gutterballs
Santa Monica Airport, Santa Monica

After being drugged by Jackie Treehorn, the Dude has a Busby Berkeley–inspired dream featuring chorine dancers wearing bowling-pin headdresses and Maude Lebowski in a Valkyrie outfit. As a bonus, Kenny Rogers provides the music. The forced-perspective set was built in a disused hangar at Santa Monica Airport.

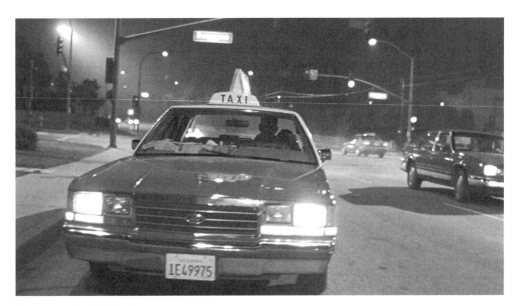

Peaceful Cab
Duquesne and Jefferson, Culver City

After a run-in with Malibu's psychotic chief of police (I believe the police station was probably a set), the Dude catches a cab back home. The only trouble is, the cabbie is listening to the Eagles, a band the Dude hates. The Dude voices this opinion, and the cabbie abruptly pulls over and throws the Dude out. This scene takes place at the intersection of Duquesne and Jefferson Streets, across from Culver City Park.

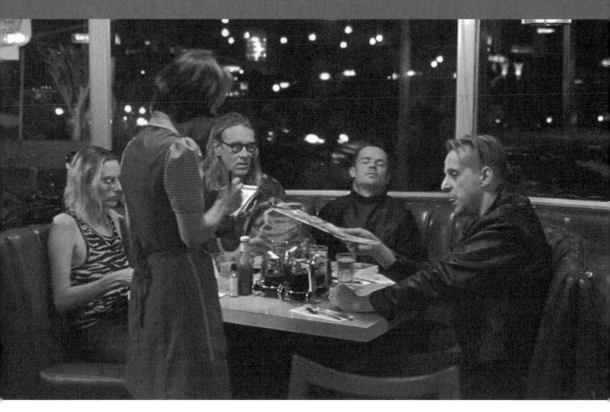

Nihilist Breakfast
Dinah's, 6521 South Sepulveda, Culver City

Just down the road from the stranded Dude, the nihilists order breakfast at Dinah's, another Googie building. Here we discover that the severed toe belongs not to Bunny, but to one of the nihilists' girlfriends (played by musician Aimee Mann).

And, yes, Dinah's actually does serve both lingonberry pancakes and pigs in a blanket.

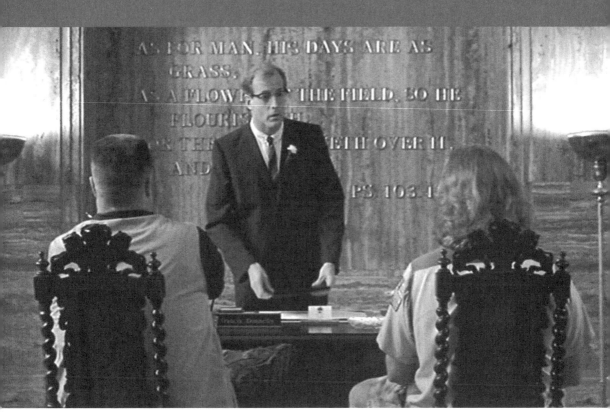

The Mortuary
Location Unknown

Poor Donny. He suffers Walter's abuse throughout the whole film only to have a heart attack and die at the end. Walter and the Dude have him cremated and then argue with the funeral director to negotiate a better rate for the "receptacle" to "transmit" his remains. I have no idea where this was filmed. Jeff Bridges says it may also have been a set.

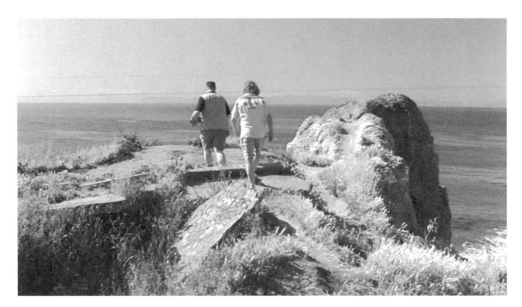

Donny's Eulogy
Somewhere along the coast of Palos Verdes

I am still trying to pinpoint the exact spot where Walter delivers his farewell to Donny before accidentally scattering most of the ashes onto the Dude. I know it to be somewhere in the ritzy Palos Verdes area somewhere. However, there is a strong possibility that the actual spot has either fallen into the sea or is privately owned. Until we know for sure, you can visit several similar spots up and down Palos Verdes Drive. The views are quite impressive from any of them.

Afterword

I first saw *The Big Lebowski* going on twenty years ago, at a press screening in one of those out-of-the-way Manhattan screening rooms. I saw it in my role as a movie critic for the *New Yorker*, a position I shared with Anthony Lane. Movie reviewing, like most writerly occupations, is a clubby business and I had the feeling from first to last that I was viewed as an outsider—as someone who hadn't climbed the necessary ladder of interim steps and thereby lacked the proper credentials—despite the fact that I had been writing about film in some form or other since my early twenties. Since I've always hated insiderness, this was fine with me and I determined to go my own way, relying on my instincts rather than checking out what other critics were saying.

I mention all this only because it seems to me that *The Big Lebowski* is in some way the quintessential insider movie, one that plays cunningly to groupthink: you're either in on the joke, or you aren't. In my case, true to the contrarian I am, I mostly resisted the joke at the time, taking the film—and its hipster directors, Joel and Ethan Coen—to task for being sophomoric, for its pose of cynical disengagement. "What's up with the Coen brothers?" I began my review, a bit incredulously. "Do their thoughts run, like Wordsworth's, too deep for words? Or do they speak a secret language of siblings, in which their meaning is clear only to each other?" Although I went on to credit the film and its creators with "an unflappable sense of visual style" and clever dialogue, I finally found the movie too self-consciously chilled out for its own good.

Well, the years have creaked by, and—who would have thunk it?—this ode to deadbeats, this lurching form of California noir (which even John Turturro, who is in the film, admits he didn't completely get when he first saw it), has gone on to acquire bona fide cult status, spawning annual Lebowski Fests with accompanying T-shirts and bumper stickers. The Dude, as it turns out, abides—and there is no such thing as being too chill. All the film's zanily obscure shenanigans are of great, even obsessive interest to its many fans, who go around quoting lines—"The rug really tied the room together" or "You're entering a world of pain" or "Shomer fucking Shabbos"—like they were ontological gems, outtakes from a shaggy-dog brand of American existentialism.

What can I say? There was nothing for it but for me to watch the movie again, with an open mind and a soupcon of indulgence. I viewed it, as it happens, on a computer screen in my sister's apartment in Jerusalem, which is where I was when I received the request to write this afterword in the company of one of my twenty-something Orthodox nephews—who, it transpired, much to my surprise, was a tried-and-true Lebowski-ite. It was a Saturday night, Yom Kippur had just ended, and I sat in the dark watching Jeff Bridges amble around exuding what I originally described as his "lazy charm," wearing his too-big shorts, and surviving all manner of real and metaphorical blows like the most resilient of cartoon characters. This time around, I found myself captivated by the Busby Berkeley sequence narrated from inside the mind of a bowling ball and admired the lush tones with which Roger Deakins, the cinematographer, manages to imbue everything, from the Dude's ratty L.A. pad to the bowling alley he frequents. The movie is more beautiful to watch than I had remembered, and I found myself more amused than irritated by the insistent laid-backness that is the heart of the film's ethos. Perhaps reality has grown more unbearable since the film was made, but the Dude and his disconnect from the real world seems like an attitude that has its distinct appeal. Not to overlook the star turns of the rest of the sterling ensemble cast, with Philip Seymour Hoffman playing an oleaginous gofer, Julianne Moore a performance-artist feminist, and Turturro a crazed, light-footed bowler. Or the ace soundtrack, which encompasses everyone from Bob Dylan to Nina Simone to Henry Mancini.

Don't get me wrong. I'm not a convert. I still think it's primarily a guys' flick, one that a little weed helps go down more smoothly. That said, it does have a loony charm. And I still love the attention that is paid to language—what I described in the *New Yorker* review as "the discrepancy between a hyper-articulate level of discourse and the dopiness of the subject at hand." Small wonder that, as the authors here note, the film's lexicon is often how its fans find one another. Meanwhile, I don't know about you, but I'm still hoping to curse someone out by calling him or her "you human paraquat." There's really no comeback to that one, is there?

Whimsically yours,
Daphne Merkin

IMAGE CREDITS

Images identified by page number are reproduced with the kind permission of the following:

Photo montage, page vi, from left to right: (row 1) Universal Studios (all); (row 2) Oliver Benjamin, Jeff Bridges, Jeff Bridges, Universal Studios; (row 3) Universal Studios, The Cartoon Network, Universal Studios, Bill Green; (row 4) Ralphs, Bill Green, Universal Studios; (row 5) Jerry Duvall, Bill Green, Jerry Duvall, Universal Studios; (row 6) Universal Studios, Jeff Bridges, Bill Green; (row 7) Jeff Bridges, Universal Studios, Jeff Bridges, Universal Studios; (row 8) Mike Walsh, Jeff Bridges, Jeff Bridges

Lew Abernathy: 106

Oliver Benjamin: 17, 137

Jeff Bridges: xii, 26, 31, 37, 41, 45, 49, 53, 57, 62, 65, 69, 72, 89, 93, 102, 120

Asia Carrera's Personal Appearance Archives/AsiaCarrera.com: 76

Cartoon Network: 148 (all). ©2007 The Cartoon Network, Inc. THE POWERPUFF GIRLS and all related characters and elements are used with the permission of and are trademarks of Cartoon Network ©2007. FOSTER'S HOME FOR IMAGI-NARY FRIENDS and all related characters and elements are used with the permission of and are trademarks of Cartoon Network ©2007.

Jason Clark: 183

Lindsey Dobson: 182 (bottom)

Brian Durkin: 182 (top)

Jerry Duvall: 172 (all), 173 (all), 174 (bottom)

Pat Evans: 218, 219 (all), 220 (all), 221 (all)

Lauren Faust: 147

Kristin Fiedler: 171 (top)

Jaik Freeman: 113

Bill Green: xi, 2 (bottom), 7, 9, 11, 13 (all), 14, 16, 74, 80, 86, 171 (bottom), 174 (top), 175, 178, 184, 185, 186, 187, 188 (all), 192

Hillary Harrison: 13 (car photo)

Hubble Heritage Team (AURA/STScI/NASA), NASA, and the NSSDC: 126 (note: NASA does not endorse this book or its contents)

LebowskiFest.com: 4, 5 (right)

Sam Matzek: 88, 95, 176, 181 (all)

John Milius: 119

Mordac.org: 5 (left), 177 (all)

Jody Morris: 143

Alysha Naples: 159

Ben Peskoe: 170 (bottom)

Joe Reifer: 179, 180 (all)

Soraya Rozkuszka: 154

Ryan Russell: 134

Will Russell: 168, 170 (top)

Ross Shannon: 150

Universal Studios: xiv, 1, 2 (top), 6, 8, 18, 19, 21, 27, 30, 33, 39, 43, 46, 51, 54, 58, 63, 66, 71, 73, 75, 77, 79, 81, 83, 87–123 (flipbook), 96, 99, 107, 118, 121, 132, 141, 144, 161, 204, 214, 215, 216, 217, 222, 223, 224, 225, 226, 227, 228, 229, 230 (all), 231, 232, 233, 234

Mike Walsh: 3, 169

USC School of Cinematic Arts: 97

White House Photo Collection: 15

Michal Zacharzewski: 10

A NOTE ON THE AUTHORS

Bill Green is a graphic designer and the poster artist for Lebowski Fest. Ben Peskoe is a web developer and writer. Will Russell, an entrepreneur, and Scott Shuffitt, an artist, are the Founding Dudes of Lebowski Fest.